T0078412

*THE ROLE OF THE SPIRIT IN THE
ESCHATOLOLOGICAL ETHICS OF REVELATION.*

BY:
PANDELANI PAUL MBEDZI

*A DISSERTATION SUBMITTED IN PARTIAL
FULFILMENT OF THE REQUIREMENTS
FOR THE DEGREE OF MISTER IN
LITERATURE AND PHILOSOPHY*

IN BIBLICAL STUDIES NEW TESTAMENT

IN THE FACULTY OF ARTS AND PHILOSOPHY

AT THE RAND AFRIKAANS UNIVERSITY.

ADVISOR: PROF. JAN A DU RAND.

OCTOBER 1996.

THE ROLE OF THE SPIRIT IN THE ESCHATOLOGICAL ETHICS OF REVELATION

PANDELANI PAUL MBEDZI

PARTRIDGE
A Penguin Random House Company

ISBN: Hardcover   978-1-4828-0797-4
               Softcover   978-1-4828-0798-1
               eBook   978-1-4828-0796-7

Scripture quotations marked KJV are from the Holy Bible, King James Version (Authorized Version). First published in 1611. Quoted from the KJV Classic Reference Bible, Copyright © 1983 by The Zondervan Corporation.

Print information available on the last page.

To order additional copies of this book, contact
Toll Free 0800 990 914 (South Africa)
+44 20 3014 3997 (outside South Africa)
orders.africa@partridgepublishing.com

www.partridgepublishing.com/africa

CONTENTS

ACKNOWLEDGEMENT

THE FOLLOWING DESERVES MY DEEPEST GRATITUDE AND THANKS:

God who created me in His image and gave me power to think and to do. He also gave me the good health to make it through. I do not have words enough to thank Him.

To my dear wife Maureen who worked on the scrip around the clock to try and meet deadlines. She edited, typed and saw it to the finish. She deserves many thanks.

To my loving kids, Tsiko, Thikho and Tshidzwa who understood when they were told, "I am busy, ask mom".

To professor, Dr. Jan A Du Rand, who mastered the art of being kind and positive even if it was tough for me? He believed in me as a student and that kept me going. He deserves the greatest thanks.

My parents Suzan and Alfred for the molding of my character. And to the Church at Montshiwa who gave me courage to go on. To Solly Kubheka my Co-worker and his family who worked for me in my absence.

To Mrs. Chinonge my- sister – in – law who with a soft voice encouraged me to finish. To her boys Christopher and Kakeya.

To Mr. Jack Sampisi and his wife who picked my kids in my absence and for his understanding when I say I am going to be RAND AFRIKAANS UNIVERSITY. To them I say, thank you very much, may the Lord richly bless you.

SUMMARY

The role of the spirit in the Eschatological Ethics of Revelation was a topic that has given me Great Joy to learn the book of Revelation the role of the Spirit, Eschatological and Ethics. In this book I have discovered the plan of Salvation which was laid before the foundation of the World in a very clear manner. God, The Master of the universe, revealed to John the final story of this world's history, at the Isles of Patmos.

The Trinity is well explained and even their duties as the God Head. God the Father, God the Son and God the Holy Ghost of which my dissertation is looking at the office or the role of the Spirit in the Second Coming of Christ. From Genesis to Malachi, it is God the Father who revealed Himself to mankind, and from Matthew to Acts 1:8., it is God the Son who came in person to reveal God the Father and from Acts 1:9 to Revelation it is God the Holy Spirit who will teach us all that God the son could not finish teaching us.

The script is divided into five chapters which are the orientation into the book of Revelation, the theology and the ethics of the book Revelation, the Eschatology Ethics in Revelation, the Holy Spirit in Revelation and the Role of the Spirit and Eschatology Ethics of Revelation, which is the theme of this script. Then we have the conclusion of the script.

There are very few books written on Revelation and let alone on the Spirit but I have tried to outline the role of the Spirit in this great book of the bible and I hope to research further on some issues that are in Revelation. It is the book that summaries the history of the world kingdoms in only 22 chapters and I have limited mine to only five chapters. The Spirit has played the greatest role in Revelation because to plan it is the time for it to play its role. The last events of this world will be shocking, the devil is angry.

In the book of Revelations God calls Himself as King of Kings and Lords of Lords. He is the Almighty God. All creation owns their existence to Him. It was one book of the Bible I did not like reading, but the research has helped me to develop some liking for the book. It the book for our modern generation and unlike the book of Daniel which was to be put away until the end times, this one is to be read and a blessing is pronounce to the one who will read the book. We need to read this book very much and books that are in context should be written about the book. The few books that have been written on Revelation are not all very relevant. They miss the point. Most of them need well researched books to make clear the mysteries that are in Revelation and the Bible explains itself even in other books of the Bible which can also be used to explain the book of Revelation. The book of Daniel even though it's in the Old Testament, it has a lot in common with the book of Revelation.

The book of Revelation opens for the reading of the book of Daniel in the Old Testament and for one to understand Revelation well; one needs to read the book of Daniel together with Revelation. The beasts in Daniel are the beasts in Revelation. Even though some people would want to divide the old and the New Testament, they are the same and they interpret each other very well. The New Testament has a lot of Old Testament quotations.

I am trying to correct some misinterpretation of some verses found in the Book of Revelation and it will be good for any one who will read this script to read it carefully and critically because in the field of learning we learn by making mistakes and your input will be appreciated. In Revelation the devil is being given the last warning and all those that need life are called to come out of Babylon the Mother of all Harlots because if we do not come out of her and keep the commandments of God, then we will drink of the wrath of God which will be poured without a mixture for all those that worship the beast and its image.

The events which are described in the book are challenging and very scaring because they talk about the future of the world and the future of the world affects me and you directly, whether we care or not. The book calls all that are off – guard to be on guard because very soon the King of this world will be coming and He will end the suffering of His followers and bring destruction to the followers of the devil and the worshipers of the beast.

We are called to make a decision which will affect us as individuals and as a group. We have to choose between

God and the Devil and we are called to be conquerors because Christ who is the Lion of Judah has overcome the Devil in heaven and at the cross of Calvary. All those who follow Him are promised the victory over sin. God does not force any one, He says, I stand at the door and knock and whosoever opens, He says, I will come in and sup with him. Life eternal is promised to all who will overcome.

The danger will follow all those who will choose not to follow Him, because the lake of fire is prepared for the Devil and his angels and all those that worship the beast and his image (666). This is eternal doom and destruction. He that has an ear let him hear what the Spirit says to the churches. We are warned of the coming danger and the world does not seem to see or know the impending danger. When the flood came, the whole world was found not ready, except eight people. The birth of Christ was also witnessed by a few shepherds and a wise man. While the teachers of the law were found not ready and yet they had their Bibles in their hands. His coming will also find a lot of people unprepared including the Professors of theology. The question is, will it be you or me who is going to be left out or not?

Let us study the book of Revelation together so that we may be ready. We are leaving in an information age and we have no excuse for not knowing the truth. If we get lost it will be through rebellion not ignorance. The devil knew what was right, but he chooses to do the wrong things and he is expelled from heaven. He does not want to go to hell alone, he wants company.

DECLARATION

I hereby declare that the dissertation submitted for the magister in biblical studies in New Testament degree to the Rand Afrikaans University, apart from the help recognized, is my own work and has not been formerly submitted to another university for a degree.

CHAPTER 1

Orientation: Authorship, Date Literature, Purpose and Structure of Revelation

In this chapter, I am going to give a little summary of the authorship, date, literature, purpose and structure of the book of Revelation. I must emphasize however, that this will not be an exhaustive study. The book of Revelation needs thorough study and more research in our day than ever before. There are very few relevant books written on Revelation and it is a very complicated book of the bible because of the images and beasts found in it.

1   Authorship

The Revelation of Jesus Christ is unique among the books of the Bible – unique in its form, its symbolism, and its meaning. The question about the possible authorship of Revelation to John is determined by the context of the origin of the writing and it offers a historical perspective which places the understanding of Revelation in relief. According to Du Rand: "Various possibilities of authorship have already been mentioned." (Du Rand 1991:221). John the Elder is a greater possibility.

1.1 John the Elder

There is little question concerning the authorship's identity. Four times He calls himself John and declares he has previously borne record of the word of God. The fourth gospel, three Epistles and the Apocalypse bear his name. eusebius, speaks of John the Elder as the author of revelation who was well known in Ephesus, "possibly being identified with the Ephesians school". (Anderson Roy 1953:1).

The above evidence proves that John is the author. While some may still doubt his authorship, it has been accepted from the earliest times. John the elder had authority in the earlier church. According to Anderson, "He was the first person in church history to be known as theologos, 'the theologian". (Ray Anderson 1953:2). John wrote as an authority to the churches.

The following statement by a scholar of a century ago sums up the position:

> "There is scarcely a book in the whole bible whose genuineness and inspiration were more strongly attested on its first appearance than the apocalypse. No doubt whatsoever seems to have entertained on these points. Suffice it now to say, that Papias, Justine, Martyr, Irenaeus, Melito, - that is, eminent teacher in the church, in the next age to that in which it was written – proclaim that its writer was then the voice of the church", - Chr. Wordsworth, Lectures on the apocalypse, page 22. Quoted by (Anderson 1953:2)"

Irenaeus is the first writer who ascribed the authorship of Revelation and John's gospel to John the son of Zebedee. Irenaeus spent his youth in Smyran. Du Rand says "The testimony of Irenaeus was taken over and chained by Hippolytus, Tertullian and origin, and this was the traditional view point of the church until the phase of historical interpretation" (Du Rand 1991:221-222).

1.2   The Disciple of Jesus Christ

John the beloved disciple of Jesus Christ is the one who wrote the apocalypse. Justin the martyr who lived for some time in Ephesus (CA 135 CE), however declared unequivocally in his dialogue with Trypho that "Revelation was written by John, one of the apostles of Christ" (Du Rand 1991: 221).

Tradition has it that, John the disciple was the sole survivor of the original apostles, everyone of the others having met a martyr's death. John was summoned to Rome to appear before the Emperor Domitian. The last of the twelve great Caesars, to be tried for his faith.

It is said:

> "So convincing was his defense that his hearse was astonished at his wisdom and eloquence. They could not gainsay his testimony. The Emperor, filled with rage ordered that he be cast into a caldron of boiling oil. But the Lord preserved the life of his faithful servant, even as he preserved y– 70).

When John survived the boiling oil he was sent to the Island of Patmos for imprisonment and then God showed him visions while there. God is God of time and history and He reveals it to whosoever He wills e.g. Daniel and John received the visions.

1.3 Another John

There are those who claim that the book of Revelation is a pseudonymous writing. The writer claims to be John, the mention of John's name will give the book the authority. If Revelation is a pseudonymous writing, the question is why did the author neglect to make it agree more closely to the gospel according to John? "The author of Revelation does not have a style or touch of a pseudonymous authorship." (Du Rand 1991:225).

Some claim John Mark as another possible candidate, but he only accompanied Paul once and there is no historical link for him with the western part. He is not a possible candidate.

Another possibility was John, the presbyter, who also lived in Asia, according to tradition. Dionysus affirms that there are two tombs ascribed to John. The use of John's name in the book, the author supposes that the readers would know who John is. He had already written other books and he did not any introduction. John the presbutos is not known and the arguments used will not convince anyone. Some say John the Baptist could be the author, but he died while Jesus was still on earth.

In conclusion we know that John was Christian apocalyptic prophet, who knew the seven congregations of Asia Minor well. John's decent is largely Jewish on the basis of his emphasis on the old and new testament in Revelation. His knowledge of Jewish traditions and symbolism and the similarities with the Jewish apocalypse as regards form and content underscore this. John the elder, the disciple of Jesus Christ qualifies to be the author.

1.4   John the Revelator

The first chapter tells us that the author is John and he was writing the Revelation of Jesus Christ. It originated with God the father, then Jesus Christ, his angel, then the prophet John in a vision and John revealed it to us. He is the author.

1.5   Structure on Formal Level

There are some similarities on the writings of revelation and the gospel of John and the letters. According to Du Rand he sees the prologue in all the writings as unique in the New Testament because the books are using similar vocabulary and style. On the formal level Du Rand says:

> "As regards to theology and terminology, similarities with the letters and the Gospel of John can possibly be there, according to certain theories, indicate a common apostolic authorship with all these writings. The following are the most important: the use of Logos for Christ (In 1:1) (Rev 9:13); Christ the Lamb (Arnion in Revelation and Amnos in the

gospel of John); Christ is a shepherd (Cf in10: If, 21:16 f with Rev7:17); Manna (In 6:31 f, Rev 2:17); quotations from the old Testament (In 19:37, Rev 1:7), and the Antitheses to mention a few". (Du Rand 1991: 222).

There are Theological and other differences between the Gospel of John and Revelation which should not be over looked. In Revelation the doctrine of God is focused on His creation and on the execution of judgement, on the other hand the gospels focus on God's love. Christological in Revelation reveals Christ as a conquering Messiah who rules with an iron rod, whilst in the gospels He is the revealer of the Father. According to Du Rand, "the gospel concentrates more on the realized eschatology over against the emphasizes on the future dimension in Revelation." (Du Rand 1991:222)

1.6   Structure on Content Level

Revelation reveals Jesus Christ in prophecy, and the gospels in his earthly life, Ministry, suffering, death, resurrection and ascension. In revelation Christ is pictured in glory at the right hand of God as high priest and Minister of the heavenly sanctuary. Anderson calls it "The Revelation about Jesus Christ" (Anderson 1953:3).

Christ is the centre of John's gospel, the three Epistle and the book of Revelation and because of the same trend of thought, John the Elder could be the author of Revelation, but there are those who do not agree that the book of

Revelation was written by the same John who wrote the epistles and the gospel.

The objections are as follows: If John wrote Revelation he must have been very old. So it would have been impossible at such an advanced age to write. However the argument is very relative. Some texts claim that John, the son of Zebedee, could have died a martyr's death before 70 Ce. John the Revelator does not claim to be one of the apostles and does not say anything about Christ's life on earth in Revelation accept in the other books.

Dionysuns, the Bishop of Alexandria in Egypt claims that it was not John of the gospel because of the language and style. Dionysus's opinion is that another John wrote the book of Revelation. It is said that if John was not the author, the book will not receive recognition in the East. Others say that it was a well known tendency to ascribe all writings to the apostles and John was a common name.

Du Rand says "the book of Revelation from the above survey can be concluded that it is not forgone conclusion that according to this information, John the apostle, the son of Zebedee could have written the book: (Du Rand 1991:224).

2 Date

It is very important to determine the dating of the book of Revelation because this will help us understand the content contextually. We will also understand certain historical, spiritual and social realities of the situation which are reflected in the imagery and narration. The dating will open a lot of hidden historical background of the book of Revelation.

Scholars date Revelation towards the end of emperor Domitian, around A.D 94 to 96. Domitian was Emperor from 81 – 96 CE. There are yet other scholars who date the book to 68 – 69 CE. John's vision in Revelation 2:2 about the new Jerusalem suggest that the old one had been destroyed in 70 CE and it will put the date after the destruction of the temple

Victorinus and Eusebius mentioned John's banishment to Patmos during the reign of Domitian. This information can cast light on the socio – historical circumstances of the writer and readers of Revelation. We have already discussed the dates of Domitian's rule above and it will be easy to determine it from the clue until the contrary is proven, we can regard the dating of Irenaeus as an important clue.

Historically both Nero and Domitian persecuted Christians. Mrs. Ellen White also supports it in the book of Acts of the Apostles. Domitian enjoyed emperor veneration, the Christians were persecuted because they could not worship the emperor. Du Rand says "The Christians' exclusive worship of the only God, through Jesus Christ, did not even leave room for the veneration of the emperor." (Du Rand 1991:232).

I would like to conclude dating as follows: Irenaeus has a strong argument and he dates Revelation at the end of the reign of Domitian (CA 95 – 96). This is the ideal date. I would like to concur with Du Rand and other scholars that taking everything into consideration, a dating of Revelation (95 – 96 CE) during the reign of Domitian, "according to the testimony of Irenaeus in Asia minor, offer a suitable frame work within which the message can be read and understood." (Du Rand 1991: 234).

3   The Type of Literature

The opening verse of Revelation tells us what kind of literature the book belongs to. There are about three kinds of literature in Revelation:

1) It is a revelation or "apocalypse".
2) Revelation is a prophecy (Rev. 1:3).
3) Revelation is intended to be a letter and it has the usual form of a letter.

According to Bauckham, the opening verses of Revelation seem to indicate that it belongs not to just one but three kinds of literature. The first verse, which is virtually a title, speaks of the Revelation of Jesus Christ, which God gave Him and which reaches God's servants through a chain of Revelation: God- > Christ -> Angel -> John (the writer) -> the servants of God.

3.1   An Apocalyptic Literature

Apocalyptic literature is often the results of a social crisis. The book of Daniel, Ezra, Baruch are all examples of writings written during or after an intense crisis for the Jewish people. In the book of Revelation you will find a trace of crisis on the Christians who were leaving in Asia Minor at the church which received the seven letters.

According to Du Rand, John's selection of forms, images and motifs from his religious tradition are very closely related to the historical and social situation in which Revelation originated. "The conflicts with Judaism, the heathen environment and Rome are of the most important factors forming the socio – historical context." (Du Rand 1991:235).

When you read Revelation you will discover that it is an apocalyptic prophecy in the form of a circular letter to the seven churches in the Roman province of Asia Minor (Rev 1:11). We therefore need to do justice to the three categories of literature – apocalypse, prophecy and letter into which Revelation seems to fall.

3.1.1 Revelation as Christian Prophecy

John was a Jewish Christian prophet. He had one rival of a false prophetess, whose name was Jezebel. Since Christian worship meetings is where a prophet prophesied, we must also assume that this is what John normally did, but since he was a prisoner in Patmos, he sent prophetic writings in a letter form to be read to his congregations. John received a vision and reported to the churches as prophecy.

The whole book of Revelation is a report of visionary revelation, but it also includes Oracular prophecy within it. John had a double Job of proclaiming the past prophecy within it. John had a double Job of proclaiming the past prophecies and his own prophecies. (Rev 10:8-11). He wrote in the climax of Prophecy, "when all the eschatological oracles of the prophets are about to be finally fulfilled, and so he interprets and gathers them up in his own prophetic revelation". (Baukham 1993:5)

John is a Christian prophet because he talks of Old Testament prophetic fulfillment which have come and gone. These prophetic expectations were in the victory of the lamb. The messenger of God was commissioned to prophecy about Christ, so the description fits him, that of a Christian prophet.

3.1.2 Revelation as an Apocalypse

Bible scholars have long distinguished between Old Testament prophecy and that of Jewish apocalypse, which includes Daniel, 2 Baruch of the old testament books etc. The difference between prophecy and apocalypses can be debated.

J.J. Collins as quoted by Bauckham defines the literacy genre apocalypse in this way

> 'Apocalypse is a genre of revelatory literature with a narrative framework, in which a revelation is mediated by another worldly being to a Human recipient, disclosing a transcendent reality which is temporal, insofar as it envisages eschatological salvation, and spatial, insofar as it involves another, supernatural world'. (Bauckham 1993:6).

Some scholars limit apocalypse to history and eschatology, but we should not because the Jewish apocalypse does not limit itself to that alone but covers a wide range of topics. John's apocalypse is exclusively concerned with eschatology, thus with eschatological judgement and salvation and the impact of the present situation in which he writes. John's work is prophetic apocalypse in that it communicates a disclosure of a transcendent perspective on this world. 'He is given a glimpse behind the scenes of history so that he can see what is really on in the events of his time and place."(Bauckham 1993:7).

John's visions were to open the reader's world into the eschatological future and to divine transcendence. The word apocalypse is translated Revelation in English what can be revealed is what is hidden. A blessing is pronounced to everyone that will read the apocalypse. (Rev.1:3).

3.1.3   Revelation as a Circular Letter

The whole book is a circular letter addressed to seven specific churches. From Patmos a preacher will go to Ephesus, Smyrna, Pergamum, Thytira, Sardis, Philadelphia and Laodicea. Though the letters were written to these churches, the message is applicable to modern churches today. The entire world history is revealed by the book of Daniel and Revelation.

A circular can speak even to those it was not addressed to; only when something of the context of its original addresses become part of the way it speaks to them. To each church

Jesus makes a promise of eschatological salvation. Each church is called to be victorious in the letter.

In revelation seven is a number of completeness. By addressing seven churches John indicates that his message is addressed to specific churches as representative of all the churches. This supported by a prophetic oracle-which occurs in each of the seven messages "let anyone who has an ear listen to what the spirit is saying to the churches". (2:7, 11, 17, 29; 3:6, 13, 22). (Bauckham 1993:16).

3.2   Revelation as a General Religious Tract

Revelation is directed to the whole Christian church. Robert Mounce says, "perhaps more than any other book in the new Testament, (apocalypse) enjoyed wide distribution and early recognition. Though addressed to the seven churches within a short while it was read throughout the province. "(Mounce 1977:36)

There was a time in history where scholars avoided the books of Daniel and Revelation from their syllabus in theological universities. Today the two books are the most studied books of the bible. In the bible there is prophecy about the knowledge that shall increase, and it has because people are studying today. We are fulfilling the prophecy as we study the two books.

3.3   Revelation as a Circular

Apocalypse is a circular letter to all the churches then and now. It is prophecy and a revelation about the future events.

It is a circular that reveals the trinity, the victory which Christ had over the devil and his angels. It is an assurance for the saints that even if they go through hardship in this life if they overcome like their Lord they are going to rule with Christ for a moment and they will soon be over. We will be going home soon.

3.4   Revelation as a Commentary

The book of Revelation is very different from the New Testament books in language and style. If Revelation is a commentary, it is for the book of Daniel. The imagery in Revelation is like the one of Daniel in the Old Testament. The two books are twins they need to be studied together for clarity.

While Daniel was supposed to be a closed book, Revelation is an open book and it has opened for the reading of the book of Daniel. In Revelation there is hope for this hopeless world. In Daniel we know that every Kingdom shall come to pass and the only one that shall stand forever is the Kingdom of God. All books of the Bible begin and end in Revelation. In Genesis paradise is lost and in Revelation Paradise is regained. Therefore Revelation is a commentary not only for the book of Daniel but also for all the books of the Bible.

3.5   Theological Perspectives

The theology of Revelation is God centred. The theology of God in the book has its greatest contribution in the New Testament theology. The book was written though crisis and anticipation of consequent widespread persecution. John's message of hope will be heard by Christians who in their measure are experiencing tribulation. Bauckham says, "Our study of it must begin with God and will both constantly and finally return to God." (Bauckham 1993:23). The trinity is well explained in the book of Revelation and Their duties as the God head.

3.5.1 God

In heaven John saw a throne, and one seated on it like the ancient of days, who is God and He dominates the book of Revelation. The throne is the symbol of His almighty power. He is creator and king of creation. He has total respect for His creation. Creation sings God's praises. The present world is not at peace with God. One day God will act to destroy evil completely. He has acted, through one weapon which is the cross completely. He has acted, through one weapon which is the cross to destroy evil. God will destroy evil completely through fire.

John's view is dualistic: a universe divided, in conflict, between good and evil. The outcome is not doubtful. Evil, even in its most potent guises, is subject to the sovereign power of good – The one seated on the throne.

When God introduced himself to John he said that he is the Alpha and the Omega. (1:8) and when he concluded He declares the eschatological accomplishment of his purpose for his whole creation by saying,' it is done! (21:6) this is God the almighty in his throne room in heaven.

3.5.2   The Lamb

John saw the lamb emerging in a dramatic context. In the vision of the throne –room, John was looking for the lion of Judah. What met his gaze was "a lamb standing as though it has been slain". (5:5-6). John addressed Christ as the lamb throughout the book of Revelation. In the book of John Christ is called the lamb too.

Jesus is the lamb that was slain. Paul says: "We preach Christ and him crucified… Christ the power of God and the wisdom of God. For the foolishness of God is wiser than men, and the weakness of God is stronger than man."(1 Cor.1:23 – 25). The lamb was worthy to receive all power (5:12). As one worthy of honour side by side with the one on the throne. The lamb knocks at he door of each one's heart, he will come in if invited (3:2).

Weather praise or blame, there is manifest of pastoral concern. The flaming eyes of the lamb see with the penetrating of a caring God. The lamb declares, "I am the first and the last, and the living one. I was dead, and see, I am alive forever and ever; and I have the keys of death and Hades." (Bauckham 1993:54).

3.5.3   The Symbolic World

The world of symbols in Revelation is a very common one and God uses it to communicate to his chosen ones and we need to study very carefully and prayerfully the book of Revelation. This book is like the book of Daniel in the Old Testament and together they form such a wonderful combination to be studied together as a unit because even their symbolisms are the same and they have similar prophetic language.

3.5.3.1   Angels

God and the world evoke the heavenly world. Angels are citizens of that world. In Rev 1:1, the Revelation of Jesus Christ was made known by an angel who was sent. The rest of Revelation, angels will appear abundantly on every page. They are in thousands (5:11). Angels in Revelation play a role that is literary mediatory in the dramatic unfolding of God's plan for His world.

3.5.3.2   The Dragon

Against the lamb stands the beast, which is represented by Rome. Over against the one on the throne stands the dragon. He is called the Devil and Satan. He works against God and this world is in sin because of the Devil, the Dragon, the Deceiver.

The Devil has been overpowered in heaven by Jesus and here on earth. But he is still trying on earth. Harrington says,

> "Exiled from this heaven as a results of Jesus' victory on the cross (12:10 – 11). He returns to earth in wrath to wage war on the children of the woman. (12:12 – 17). The instrument of his warfare is the Beast (Rome) with its satellite Beasts (the imperial cult) (CH. 13)". (Harrington 1993:29).

The Dragon has the kings of this world on his side and he is going to wage war with the saints of God through the rulers of this world. He will give them power for the final battle and we need to hold fast because it won't be long Jesus will come after the great war between the devil and the saints of God.

3.5.3.3   Liturgy

Revelation is explicitly meant for public reading in a liturgy (Rev 1:3). Most likely a Eucharistic liturgy. Worship unites heaven and earth. The object of worship is nobody else excepts the one on the throne and the lamb. The voices in heaven blend with the earthly in worship. It is said, "worshiping God and the lamb will hasten the coming of the new heaven and earth were righteousness dwells" (Harington 1993:29).

3.5.3.4   Preaching

If you want to understand Revelation, read all of it one sitting or ask someone who can read it well to read it for you in one sitting. The original people who received the letter heard all of it read to them. Revelation has dramatic dimensions. Revelation must be read as a whole. The author of Revelation wrote it in a dramatic manner and the readers may not read like a novel, but if you can get a good preacher to preach to you then you can enjoy the book of Revelation.

3.6   Pastoral Written Communication in Situation

There was a crisis among the churches in Asia Minor, thus the birth of Revelation. "There were conflicts with

Judaism, the heathen environment and Rome." (Du Rand 1991: 235). The order of Rome was that any religion outside Roman religion or Judaism was illegal. "The Jewish war (66 – 70) CE.), the destruction of Jerusalem (70 CE) and the banishment from the synagogue of the eighteen prayers with the 12th one directed to heretics brought a rift between Jews and Christians." (Du Rand 1991:235). Nero blamed the Christians for the fire in Rome in (64 CE) and Jewish incitement influenced him to carry out the persecution of the Christians.

John found himself exiled in Patmos because of the word of God and the Testimony of Jesus. John was given a life long exile. Christians were willing to go martyrdom for the testimony of Jesus. According to Du Rand's court,

> "Revelation can rightly be regarded as crisis writing in the light of the above mentioned socio-historical situation. Among others it is the religious answer of a wronged, persecuted and alienated group of Christians to the socio – political situation of the day." (1991:243).

The hope of Jesus second coming, the language, symbolism of Revelation reveals the tension which was there. They had convictions that they were being persecuted for the sake of the good news, but the hope of the coming Lord comforted them.

4 The Purpose of Revelation

The apocalypse was written as a great concern for the small community of Christians in Asia Minor. John wanted to reveal to them God and Christ's victory over evil and sin. He wanted them to know that Rome was being used by the Devil and they should not swim with the tide. Rome mixed paganism and Christianity.

According to Harington, "John saw with prophetic conviction, that something was rotten at the heart of Rome. His was a firmly dualistic vision". (Harington 1991:13). John wrote to warn the Christians about the coming danger and to encourage Christians to stand firm in their love of God and to even die for the word because he who overcomes shall be rewarded with good and eternal life. John foresaw tribulation for Christians because they will resist to worship according to the powers that be.

Harington says;

> "Ironically victory is won through defeat; the victory is the victory; resistance, even passive resistance, would inevitably invite the reaction of Rome: A power based authority can break no dissension. John was urging the Christians to resistance. In the assurance that he would be heeded, he warned, repeatedly and without apology, of tribulation. After all, Christians are disciples of the slain lamb – the disciple is not greater than the master". (Harington. 1991:13).

John's purpose was to warn the world through an apocalypse of the coming danger, tribulation and to encourage Christians to be faithful until death because that has a greater reward.

When we read Revelation we get the encouragement to know that we are not alone in the struggle. We are encouraged to do good and discouraged to do wrong. We are told the enemy is angry and will soon persecute the woman and child, but we must be strong because Jesus is coming with a reward for those who will over come. Forewarned is forearmed. So be ready, he who promised will not delay, but will come soon.

5   Structure of Revelation

The structure of the book of Revelation reveals and portrays what kind of book apocalypse is. The basic structural question is whether John intended his readers to understand the visions recorded in his writings in a straight forward and chronological sense or, whether some form of recapitulation is involved.

I am going to follow the structure by Du Rand and R. H. Mounce.

5.1. Outline By R.H. Mounce.(P. 47 – 49) and Du Rand (P. 300 – 302).

Introduction	(1:1 – 20)
Preface	(1:1 – 3)
Letter Salutation	(1:4 – 6)
Theme of the book	(1:7 – 8)
Vision of call	(1:9 – 10)

1) Seven letters to the congregations (2:1 - 3: 20).
1.1. To Ephesus (2: 1 – 7)
1.2. To Smyrna (2: 8 – 11)
1.3. To Pergamum (2:12 – 17)
1.4. To Thyarita (2:18 – 29)
1.5. To Sardis (3:11 – 16)
1.6. To Philadelphia (3:7 – 13)
1.7. To Laodicea (3:14 – 22)

2) Seven seals (4:1 – 8: 5)
2.1. Prelude in heaven (4:1 – 5: 14)
2.1.1. The heavenly throne room (4:1 – 11)
2.1.2. The scroll with the seven seal and the lamb (4:1 – 14)
2.2. The opening of the seven seals (6:1 – 8:5)
2.2.1. The first four seals (6:1 – 8)
2.2.2. The fifth seal: martyrs under the alter (6:9 – 11)
2.3. The protection of God's people (7: 1 – 17)
2.3.1. The 144 000 sealed ones (7:17)
2.3.2. The great multitude before the throne (7: 9 – 17)
2.4. The seven seals opened (8:1 – 5)

3) Seven trumpets (8:6 – 11:19)
3.1. The first four trumpets (8:6 – 13)
3.2. The fifth trumpet (9:1 – 12)
3.3. The sixth trumpet (9:13 – 21)
3.4. The protection of the people of God (10:1 – 11)
3.4.1. The angel and the opened scroll (10:1 – 11:14)
3.4.2. The measuring of the temple (11:1 – 2)
3.4.3. The two witnesses (11:3 – 14)
3.4.4. The seventh trumpet (11:3 – 14)

4) The dragon and the lamb (12:1 – 14:20)

4.1. The woman, the dragon and the child (12:1 – 6)

4.2. The battle between Michael and the dragon (12:13 – 18)

4.3. The dragon war against the woman (12:13 – 18)

4.4. The beast from the sea, the Antichrist (13:11 – 18)

4.5. The beast from the earth, the false prophet (13:11 – 18)

4.6. The lamb and his redeemed (14:1 – 5)

4.7. Judgment announced, harvest gathered (14:6 – 13)

4.7.1. The announcement of judgment (14:14 – 16)

4.7.2. The son of man on the white cloud (14:14 – 16)

5) Seven bowls (15:1 – 16:21)

5.1. The prelude in heaven (15:1 – 8)

5.2. The first four bowls (16:1 – 9)

5.3. The fifth bowl (16:12 – 16)

5.4. The sixth bowl (16:12 – 16)

5.5. The seventh bowl (16:17 – 21)

6) The fall of Babylon (17:1 – 19:10)

6.1. The immoral woman on the beast (17:1 – 6)

6.2. The meaning of the woman and the beast (17:6 – 14)

6.3. The fall of the immoral woman (17:15 – 18)

6.4. The fall of Babylon announced (18:1 – 8)

6.5. Mourning over the fall of Babylon (18:9 – 20)

6.5.1. The kings weep (18:9 – 10)

6.5.2. The Merchants weep (18:11 – 17)

6.5.3. The seaman weep (18:17 – 20)

6.6. Te fall of Babylon completed (19:21 – 24)

6.7. Rejoicing over the fall of Babylon (19:1 – 10)

6.7.1. Joy in heaven (19:1 – 4)

6.7.2. The wedding of the lamb announced (19:5 – 10)

7)   Victory and new creation (19:11 – 22:5)

7.1.   The appearing of Christ (19:11 – 16)

7.2.   The beast and the false prophet conquered (19:17 – 21)

7.3.   The dragon bound for a thousand years (20:1 – 6)

7.4.   Satan is conquered (20:7 -10)

7.5.   The last judgment (20:7 – 10)

7.6.   The new creation (21:1 – 8)

7.7.   The heavenly Jerusalem (21:9 – 22:5)

7.7.1.   The Bride of the Lamb (21:9 – 14)

7.7.2.   The new Jerusalem measured and described (21:15 – 21)

7.7.3.   The new humanity (21:22 – 27)

7.7.4.   The new Paradise (22:1 – 5)

CONCLUSION (22:6 – 21)

The angel : The words are trustworthy (22:6 – 11)

Jesus   : The words are trustworthy (22:12 – 17)

John   : The words are trustworthy (22:18 – 21)

There are many structures that are followed on the book of Revelation but I have chosen Mounce and Du Rand because they are much easier to follow than the other authors I have read. When studying the structure of Revelation according to Du Rand. It is important to consider the expression "By the Spirit" (En Pneumatic) more closely. The following occurrences are just too striking to neglect when studying the structure of Revelation:

1:10	-	On the Lord's Day I was in the spirit ......
4:2	-	At once I was in the Spirit ......
17: 3	-	carried me away in the Spirit ......
21:10	-	And He carried me away in the Spirit ......

I would be discussing the role of the Spirit in the following chapters and these verses will be discussed in depth because they are the main sources of my dissertation.

CHAPTER 2

Theology and Ethics in Revelation

2 Theology of Revelation

Introduction

The book of Revelation is a work of profound theology. The book is open to all kinds of misinterpretations. It is the book of images, theology and it reveals the future of this world's history. It also calls on Christians to confront the political idolatries of the times and calls God's children in His kingdom. Revelation has relevance for today. We will also discuss the ethical issues found in the book which are vital for our salvation and our redemption.

2.1 Reading the Book of Revelation

The word "Revelation" or "Apocalypse" (Apocalypses) points the book to the Jewish genre of old Jewish and Christian literature which is called apocalypses by modern scholars. Revelation is a prophecy to be read aloud in Christian worship (Rev a:3). It is also a letter. We have already discussed the three categories of literature – apocalypse, prophecy and letter in chapter 1 and we won't dwell much on the kind of literature in this chapter. When reading the book of Revelation these three kinds of literature must be understood in order not to fall in the trap of misinterpreting the book as many have done it and are still doing it today.

The world seems to be ruled by evil, not by God. The righteous are suffering, and the wicked flourish. John's apocalypse shows the coming kingdom and the destruction of evil and the wicked. The devil seems to be lord of this world, but God will prove that He is the Lord and God of this world. God is patient with us and with evil, so that when He destroys evil He may be a good judge.

2.2   The Trinity Inrevelation

The study of Revelation begins with God will finally return to God. The one who is and who was and who is to come, the almighty. The divine trinity is so well depicted in John's work. Richard Bauckham says that the three fold terms are so clear:

> "Grace to you and peace from Him who is who was and who is to come, and from the seven spirits who are before his throne, and from Jesus Christ, the faithful witness, the first born from the dead, and the ruler of the kings of the earth." (1:4b – 5a) (Backham 1993: 23).

The theology of the book of Revelation reveals God the father, the Son and the Holly Ghost in a remarkable way. This is the theology of the trinity, in which we will follow the order: God, Christ, Spirit.

2.2.1 The Alpha and the Omega (God the Father)

The ending of the prologue of Revelation has divine self – declaration: "I am the Alpha and the Omega", says the Lord God, who is and who was and who is to come, the almighty. (1:8). The three of four designation of God stands out so well in Revelations. God speaks about Himself twice in Revelation and the quoted statements are said by God about Himself. The second occasion (21:5 – 8) includes a similar divine self declaration "I am the Alpha and the Omega, the beginning and the end" (21:6). Jesus Christ has two self – declarations which are having the same pattern:

God	:	I am the Alpha and the Omega (1:8)
Christ	:	I am the first and the last (1:17)
God	:	I am the Alpha and the Omega, the beginning and the ending (21:6)
Christ	:	I am the Alpha and the Omega, the first and the last, the beginning and the end (22:13)

There are three phrases of self – designation which apply to God. These are the Alpha and the Omega, the First and the Last, the Beginning and the End – they can be considered equivalent. "In Greek, alpha is A and omega is Z and in English it is the first and the last" (Backham 1993: 26).

Numbers mean a lot with God. There are special numbers that God uses throughout the bible, i.e. one, three, four, seven, ten, twelve, twenty – four, twenty – eight etc. these are numbers that signify completeness. There are seven beatitudes scattered throughout the book of Revelation (1:3,

14:13, 16:15, 19:9, 20:6, 22:7, and 22:14). Full blessings will be granted to reader of Revelation.

Richard Baukham says this about God:

> "Unlike human – made gods, this God is utterly incorparable one, to whom all nations are subject, whose purpose none can frustrate. (CF. ISA. 40:12 - 26). It is precisely this exclusive monotheistic faith that determines the prophetic outlook of Revelation. Hence the unique importance of the designation "the Alpha and the Omega". God precedes all things, as their creator, and will bring all things to eschatological fulfillment. He is the origin and goal of all history. He has the first word, in creation, and the last word, in new creation. (Baukham 1993 : 27)

Baukham says the designation of God occurs with variation five times:

1:4	The one who is and who was and who is to come
1:8	The one who is and who was and who is to come
4:8	The one who is and who was and who is to come
11:17	The one who is and who was
16:5	The one who is and who was

We notice here that the form with the three tenses is used three times, two tenses twice. The Lord God Almighty, the one who sits on the throne. Besides Him there is no other

God. He is the creator of all things including the devil. God alone is to be worshiped. All come from His hands and we were meant to be good.

2.3   The Lamb of the Throne

In heaven John saw a vision of a lamb in the throne and he declared that he was the first and the last, and the living one. "I was dead and see I am alive forever and ever; and I have the keys of death and hell." (1:17-18).

The self – declaration of Jesus and of God are the same or similar.
We can repeat the logic again:

>   God: I am the Alpha and Omega (1:8)
>   Christ: I am the First and the Last (1:17)
>   God: I am the Alpha and the Omega, the Beginning and the End (21:6)
>   Christ: I am the Alpha and the Omega, the First and the Last, the Beginning and the End (22:13)

Revelation has a remarkable way of identifying the trinity and the role of the Father and the Son is in such a way that it becomes very hard to separate the father God from God the son in the above statement.

Richard Bauckham says:

>   "As we have seen, the two titles; the Alpha and the Omega the beginning and the end, used of God, designated God as eternal in relation to the

world. He precedes and originates all things, as their creator, and he will bring all things to their eschatological fulfillment." (Bauckham 1993:55).

Jesus one time said to the Pharisees that "I and my Father are one" and Revelation reveals that oneness in self – declaration by both because they overlap. God is love, Jesus is the expression of that love and the Holy Spirit is the fulfillment and the assurance of that love.

2.4   The Worship of Jesus

The angels throughout scripture have refused to be worshipped, and Jesus while in the flesh refused to be worshipped but afterwards he is God and the worship and honour due to God is also due to him. Jesus told the Jews, "Before Abraham was, "I am". In the book of John, Jesus is called the word which was with God from the beginning and nothing which is created did not originate from the word. (John 1:1 – 3).

Jesus Christ is worthy of divine worship because he is the same with the one God. The lamb that was slain is Jesus Christ our Lord and Saviour. He is addressed as Lord of lords and King of kings, the Prince of Peace, the mighty God, the everlasting father. (Isaiah 9:6).

2.5   What Christ, Does, God Does

In Revelation it is clear that what Jesus Christ does, God does. They are partners in creation and redemption. According to the gospel of John 1 nothing was created without the word. This is seen in relation with the Parousia. "In the designation of God as eternal in three tenses – "the one who is, and who was and who is to come" (1:4, 8; cf 4:8). (Bauckham 1993:63).

The suffering and the death of Christ is the key event in God's conquest of evil on earth. God and the Son are one. Bauckham says "God is related to the world not only as the transcendent Holy one, but also as the slaughtered lamb." (Bauckham 1993:65). God did not only create the world, but He also redeemed it by dying for it on the cross of Calvary.

2.6   The Victory of the Lamb and His Followers

The lamb was victorious over the devil and all those that follow the lamb are promised victory because the one they follow has been an over comer and we are assured of victory if we follow the one who has overcome. We belong to God by creation and now by redemption. We are his twice. There is no room for failure unless we do not look at the cross for our salvation and salvation is free but it cost God all He ever had.

2.6.1   Statistics

The statistics of some Christological designation will prepare us for our study of Christ's work in Revelation. The name Jesus occurs 14 times. Seven times as witness (5:13; 6:16; 7:10; 14:4; 21:22; 22:1; 22:3). The word "lamb" referring to Christ, occurs 28 times (7x4). Seven is completeness and four is the four corners of the world and it means all over the world. Complete victory of the world by the Lamb that was slain.

2.6.2   The Major Symbolic Themes

Christ has to establish God's kingdom on earth, and at present the evil one rules this world. "Salvation and judgment are a process which begins with Christ's life on earth, and ends with the parousia". (Bauckham 1993:67).

In Revelation there are three distinctive theological interpretation of Christ's work:

1) The messianic war. This is the spiritual warfare as opposed to the Jewish war which they thought Christ had come for.
2) The eschatological exodus – the Egyptian exodus is like unto the modern one from the bondage of sin to the heavenly where there shall never be sin.
3) The faithful and true witness. Jesus' victory was in dying and being resurrected from the dead. Yahweh is the only true God, the creator and the Lord of history and it is vindicated against the gods of the nations. Israel is supposed to be God's witness to the nations (Isa 43:10, 12; 44:8), that God is the only true God.

2.6.3   The Death of Christ

The death and resurrection of Christ has already won his decisive victory over evil. Chapter 5, the throne room in heaven and the scroll which had no one who qualified to open it except the Lion of Judah. In this chapter the work of Christ and the three motifs, the messianic war, the new exodus and the witness has been accomplished through Christ.

Revelation 12:11 says, "They have conquered him by the blood through of the Lamb and by the word of their testimony, for they did not cling to life even in the face of death." God does not want our divided attention, but he wants our full surrender and our total loyalty to him alone. He is a God that does not change when it suits Him and when it doesn't. he is a particular God, he has to be worshiped in his way, and not our way. He has given us the direction how we should worship him.

The death of Christ on Calvary is a big example of how particular our God is, and how he cannot change even if it cost him every thing, even his own son. In Malachi 3:6, God says, "For I Am the Lord, I change not; therefore ye sons of Jacob are not consumed." When God gives instructions, He gives full details of how it is done and how it should be continued. Haskell sums up the cross as follows:

> "To every voyager on the storm – tossed sea of life, the Lord has given a compass which, if rightly used, will safely guide him into the eternal haven of rest. It was given to our first parents at the gate of Eden, after they had admitted sin into this beautiful earth as well as into their own lives. The compass consists of the following words, which were spoken by the Lord to Satan: "I will put enmity between thee and the woman, and between thy seed and her

seed." In every heart God has planted an enmity to sin, which, if heeded, will lead to righteousness and eternal life. Any man, whatever his station or rank in life, who will absolutely follow the divine compass placed in his heart, will accept Chris as his Savior and be out into the sunlight of God's love and approval." (Haskell 1914: 19 – 20).

We have to be students in the school of Christ in order to know how to serve Him well and the compass is available and the Bible is its name. The law of God cannot be changed, that is why Jesus came to die on the cross because God could not change. It is not everyone that calls Him, Lord, Lord who will enter into heaven.

Why? Because it is not everyone that does the will of God. We do not need to go out looking for persecution, but doing the will of God will cause the world to persecute us without provoking anyone. That is why Revelation 1:3, we must read in order to be blessed. Our salvation should not be left in the hands of the priests, because a priest isn't going anywhere. Our salvation depends on Christ and we are responsible for it, not our parents or pastors or teachers nor any other person. Let him/her that has an ear hear what the Spirit say to the church today.

2.6.4   The Army of Martyrs

The seven churches of Revelation have a promise of eschatological reward to "the one who conquers" (2:7; 11, 17; 26;8; 3:5,21). Rev 5:5 – 6, reads: "to the one who conquers, I will give a place with me on my throne, just as I myself conquered and sat down with my father on His throne" (3:21) (Bauckham 1991: 76).

Stephen N. Haskell says:

> "He (God) desires that the "whole Spirit and soul and body by presented blameless unto the coming of our Lord Jesus Christ;" that the entire life of the Christian be laid upon the altar, ready to be used as the Lord directs. None can do this who do not daily accepts Christ as their sin – offering and know what it is to be "accepted in the beloved". (Haskell 1914:227).

Jesus Christ has won the victory, through the sacrificial death not by military might, so are His followers. We should be victorious through martyr's death like our Lord Jesus Christ. (Rom 12:7). Present yourselves blameless. Through Jesus we are more than conquerors. Nothing should separate us from the love of God.

2.6.5   The Unsealed Scroll

The scroll reveals how Christ's followers are to participate in the coming of God's kingdom, by witnessing, sacrifice and victory. The scroll is opened by Christ alone and given to John to eat. It is sweet in the mouth and bitter in the stomach. The world needs to hear about Jesus. We have to witness, but they may not accept our message, but we should go ahead anyway.

But it is better if they have heard it, because we will have done our part which is to tell them about the love of God and salvation that is free to us, but cost God everything. Revelation 14 is a commission of every follower of Christ and this gospel of kingdom should be preached to all and the end shall come.

2.6.6   The Two Witnesses

These are the faithful witnesses and the death of the saints which will be instrumental in the conversation of the nations of the world. God's people will be redeemed from all the nations (5:9) and will witness to all nations (11:3-13). Some claim Moses and Elijah as the two witnesses. They are symbols of victory. Moses died and so he represents those who died and will be resurrected. Elijah on the other hand was taken up to heaven and he did not die so he represents those will not see death at the coming of Jesus Christ.

There are those who claim that the two witnesses represent the old and the New Testament scriptures. Anderson in support of the Bible that it is in the two witnesses has the following to say:

> "The clearest explanation of this prophecy is that the witnesses are the Old and New Testaments. They do indeed testify of Christ. 'They are they which testify of me,' He said, John 5:39. "The two witnesses represent the scripture of the Old and New testament.

Both are important testimonies to the origin and perpetuity of the law of God. Both are witnesses also to the plan of salvation. The types, sacrifices, and prophecies of the Old and New Testaments point forward to a savior to come. The gospels and Epistles of the New Testament tell of a Savior who has come in the exact manner foretold by type and prophecy." – The Great Controversy, p.267." (Anderson 1953:108).

Some say the Bible and the Spirit of Prophecy, but I agree with those who say the Old and the New Testament because according to history, in November 1793, till June 1797 the French assembly passed a decree suppressing the scriptures. Paris became the spiritual Sodom. After three and half years the bible was freed and it was placed in honor. In 1804 the bible was exalted and the British and Foreign Bible Society was organized. Today the Bible is the most translated and the most read book in the whole world, than any other book written by mankind.

During the dark ages bibles were chained to the pulpits and no one was allowed to read them except the Priests. Many Christians were killed for translating the bible into vernacular. Those who did that were labeled as heretics. E.g. Jerome, John Huss, Martin Luther etc. We can write another book on the persecutions of saints and of the bible, because History is full of it.

2.6.6.1   The Harvest of the Earth

When all shall be brought to judgment, at the latter end of the world's history, the world will be harvested. The good seed will be taken to glory and the bad one shall remain to be burned later by fire. We must decide where we belong because the choice should be made by each individual while still living.

We are responsible for the decisions we make on this side of life and they will decide our destiny. We need to make responsible commitment so that we may have life and have it abundantly. Jesus in Isaiah 1:18, says that we should come ad reason with him, no matter how ugly our sins are, they shall be as white as snow. Harvest is sure to come but where will you be, will you be on God's side or the Devil's side?

2.6.7   The Conversion of the Nation

The book of Revelation is there so as to alert the nations so that they can be converted and follow the Lamb. There is life eternal in following the Lamb and there is death in rejecting the Lamb. God has given us the power of choice. Richard Bauckham says:

> "We now see that this redemption of a special people from all the people is not an end in itself, but has a further purpose: to bring all the people to acknowledge and worship God. In the first stage of His work the Lamb's bloody sacrifice redeemed a people for God. In the second stage, this people's participation in His sacrifice, through martyrdom,

wins all the people for God. This is how God's universal kingdom comes". (Bauckham 1993:101). (5: 9, 10).

Reading the book of Revelation is a blessing because we will come to the knowledge of God and choose to be judged as evil doers or saints. "Behold I stand at the door and knock", Christ is knocking at the door of the nations so that they may come to repentance. (Revelation 3:20).

2.6.8   The Parousia

Jesus was the faithful witness till death and he is the high priest in heaven, waiting for his second coming when He will come as "King of kings and Lords of lords" (17:14; 19:16). Jesus should come quickly to end death and misery, it is becoming like the time of Noah. The world has become so rough that it is not so easy to live here any more.

People have become like animals and killing other human beings it's like killing a fly, life has lost value so much that we have no regard for life any more. Jesus must come to release us from this suffering of this life. One prophecy after another has come to pass. We hope any day now we will be going home.

2.6.9   The Millenium

The millennium and the parousia are closely related. The millennium is the period of a thousand years in which the devil will be chained and all evil doers will be dead while the saints will be in heaven with God (Rev 20: 4 − 8).

After the millennium, the Devil will be released and the New Jerusalem will come down from God, then the final destruction will come. Fire will fall down like rain and it will eat up all who did not do the will of God, but their will or the Devil's will.

When you look at the history of this world you will see that it is six thousand years. It is divided into three periods which are as follows, the first two thousands years is from Adam to Noah's flood, the second period is from the flood to the birth of Jesus Christ, and the last period is from the birth of Christ to his second advent. The Millennium to me is the crown of this world's history, just as the Sabbath was God's crown of creation.

I believe that those who will be saved and had not had an opportunity to keep the Sabbath for one thousand years so that when we come from heaven all of us may have known what the Sabbath means to God, because today we do not know the Value of the Sabbath. This theory of mine need to be studied further.

2.7   The Spirit of Prophecy

There was a time in human history when God spoke to man face to face before sin came into the world and then he sent his son to come and die for mankind and when the son left for heaven He did not leave us alone, but he promised to send God the Holy Spirit. The Spirit of prophecy is one of the gifts of prophecy. We need it more now because false prophets have come and they claim the same spirit. The Spirit of prophecy is the testimony of Jesus. The Holy Spirit has been sent to bear testimony to Jesus and his witness is equivalent to that of Jesus in person.

2.7.1   Statistics

In the book of Revelation we find that there is reference of God ad Christ and the Holy Spirit. The third of the God Head is also mentioned. The Spirit is the one that will establish God's kingdom in the world. There are fourteen references of the Spirit in Revelation. The word "prophecy" occurs seven times in the book of Revelation.

2.7.2   The Seven Spirits

The seven spirits are the divine spirits or the seven angels. The two witnesses are mentioned also. Zachariah 4:6 says; "not by might, nor by power but by my Spirit, says the Lord of hosts". The Spirit is closely related to the Lamb and God. The Lamb is said to have "seven horns and seven eyes, which are seven spirits of God sent out into all the earth". (Bauckham 1993:112). The eyes of Yahweh are also the eyes of the Lamb in Revelation.

God and the Son now share the throne in heaven and "the seven Spirits are the presence and power of God on earth, bringing about God's kingdom by implementing the Lamb's victory throughout the world." (Bauckham 1993:113). The two witnesses do all this by the power of truth. The Old and New Testament, the Bible and the Spirit of Prophecy.

2.7.3 The Spirit of Christian Prophecy in the Churches

There are seven churches and seven Spirits in the book of Revelation and these represents the fullness of divine Spirit in relation to God, to Christ and to the church's mission to the whole world.

The churches are inspired by the Spirit to let the whole world know about the word of God. They are to let Christian's prophecy known and witness of Jesus. The coming of Christ on earth should be proclaimed in the world because it is at hand.

2.7.4 Prophecy as the Witness of Jesus

The key statement is in "the testimony of Jesus is the Spirit of prophecy" (19:10). Prophecy witnesses about Jesus. In the Old Testament it was His first coming, to die for mankind and in the New Testament it is about His second coming to redeem mankind from sin. Jesus is the theme of our salvation and of the Bible. Christians should hold the testimony of Jesus.

Bauckham says:

> "This is an acknowledgement that the role to which Revelation calls all Christians is, in essence the same as that of prophets hearing the witness of Jesus, remaining faithful in word and deed to the one true God and his righteousness" (1993:121).

The Bible says that God will never do anything without telling it to his servants the prophets. He reveals all these with His Spirit in a vision and to whomsoever He wills e.g. the wise men from the east, etc.

2.7.5   The Prophetic Message to the Churches

Prophecy addressed to the churches and the churches and the churches' prophetic witness to the world. Both the witness of Jesus and the word of God. When churches are addressed Jesus says, "I know your works". To all of them, a word of commendation or reproof is given to each of the seven churches. He who overcomes will dwell with Christ in the New Jerusalem. Behold He is coming quickly; He will come with a reward for every one.

2.8   The New Jerusalem

There are many cities in Revelation. The seven cities where the seven churches are found in Asia minor and Babylon which is evil and must fall to open way for the new Jerusalem which must come for the saved. The kings of the earth bring their glory into her (i.e. their worship and submission to God: 21:24). Babylon rules over the kings of the earth (17:18), the water of life and the tree of life for the healing of the nations (21:6; 22:1, 2) and Babylon's wine which makes the nations drunk (14:8; 17:2; 18:3).

God's people are called to come out of Babylon and enter into the New Jerusalem. Babylon means confusion and Jerusalem means the city of peace. The people of God must come out of confusion and enter into peace. There is no middle of the road, you are for God or for the Devil, but the choice is yours.

2.8.1 The New Jerusalem as a Place

It is a place on earth made new and it will come down from heaven. Bauckham describes it as follows:

> "As a place, the new Jerusalem is at once paradise, holy city and temple. As paradise it is the natural world in its ideal state, rescued from the destroyer of the earth, reconciled with humanity, filled with the presence of God, and mediating the blessings of eschatological life of humanity. As holy city, it fulfills the ideal of the anciently city, as a place where heaven and earth meet at he centre of the earth, from God rules his land and his people, to whose attraction the nations are drawn for enlightenment, and in which people live in theocentric community. As temple, it is the place where God's immediate presence, where his worshippers see his face." (Bauckham 1993:132)

The new Jerusalem is paradise because there is the water of life and the tree of life which Adam and Eve were refused to eat and will be allowed to eat of it the new city. The new Jerusalem is the theme of God's immediate presence. There is no need of a temple, no need of light there.

2.8.2   The New Jerusalem as People

It must be occupied by human beings, and God will dwell with them and they will be his people. The people who will enter the new Jerusalem are those who have overcome evil and have washed their robes in the blood of the lamb. The unrepented will be excluded from the city. Only those who will keep God's commandments will be allowed into the city.

2.8.3   The New Jerusalem as Divine Presence

God's immediate presence is the eschatological fulfillment of the new city of Jerusalem. When the new Jerusalem will come down from heaven to dwell with humans, God will wipe away every tear from their eyes (21:4). No more death, sorrow, weeping etc. man is freed from man's rule and Devil's rule. The former things shall have passed away and death will be no more and we will leave happily with God we shall live eternally.

2.9   Revelation for Today

Revelation has revealed the history and the events of this world from the time of king Nebuchadnezzar of Babylon, to the Napoleon of France, Hitler of Germany, to Great Britain, to the rulers of Russia, to the United States of America as a sole super power with no power to equal it today in the whole world. After these powers, Revelation brings in another Kingdom which will rule this world forever ad ever. That is the kingdom of our Lord Jesus Christ, the Mighty

God, the Everlasting Father, the Prince of Peace. This is the kind of Kingdom Revelation brings today.

2.9.1 The Christian Canonical Prophecy

Revelation is a prophecy and forms part of the Christian canon scripture. It has the hope for the coming of God's universal kingdom on earth. This can be seen in light of the hope of the life, death and resurrection of Jesus and the salvation of all mankind.

Revelation calls Christians to come out of Babylon which is darkness and death to the new Jerusalem which is the light and it is life eternal. It calls us from hopelessness into hope of life. The last part of this world's history will be so trying that we will long for the hope found in Revelation. The devil will be throwing the last kicks such that if it were possible even the very elect may be lost forever.

2.9.2 True Prophecy

Revelation has been accepted into the New Testament as true prophecy. When God's kingdom comes we are either going to be found in or outside the gates.

> "Biblical prophecy always both addresses the prophet's contemporaries about their own present and future immediately impending for them and raised hopes which proved able to transcend their immediate relevance to the prophet's contemporaries and to continue to direct later readers to God's purpose for the future." (Bauckham 1993:152).

2.9.3   Imminence and Delay

In the book there is tension between eschatological imminence and eschatological delay that runs through the whole apocalyptic tradition. Christians are suffering, God must come but at the same time He delays to give chance to sinners to repent. God's patience and grace. According to God everyone can be saved into the kingdom if we choose to be saved.

The imminence is hands of the saints because they are to preach the good news of salvation to the whole world then the end shall come. The delay is also in our hands because if we will not preach this good news, God will not send His Son to a world that has not heard about Jesus' coming. We have to play our part as Christians before the end shall come.

2.9.4   Revelation's Relevance Today

It is relevant today because it gives more room for study.

2.9.4.1.   It purges and refurbishes the Christian's imagination.

2.9.4.2.   It is the overwhelming concerned with the truth of God.

2.9.4.3.   It shows the power of a theocentric vision to confront oppression, injustice and inhumanity.

2.9.4.4.   It opens the world to the coming of God's kingdom. The new creation and the New Jerusalem.

2.9.4.5.   It is a liberation theology for the poor and the oppressed.

2.9.4.6.   It is in the public, political world that the Christians are to witness for the sake of God's kingdom.

2.9.4.7.   Future eschatology keeps the church oriented towards God's world and God's future for the world.

2.9.4.8.   There is true religion and false religion which we need to be careful of, The prophetic critique is for the churches and the world.

2.9.4.9.   Christians' witness and the keeping of God's commandment is very important in Revelation.

2.9.4.10. In Revelation's universal perspective, the doctrines of creation, redemption and eschatology are very closely linked.

2.9.4.11. Revelation is there, for God to be known and understood in the world. It reveals the trinity in a clear manner.

2.10   The Ethics in Revelation

Introduction

Jesus' ethical approach is that we need to have faith and works. The two cannot be separated because one cannot work without the other. The fruit of faith is good works. We cannot see faith, but we can see works that are good. Jesus did not preach the gospel of separation but the gospel of unity between Jews, the poor and the educated. He told his disciples to be fishers of men from Judea, Jerusalem,

Samaria and the utmost parts of the world. This is the good news of salvation.

The early church was a community of witness and service, a church for God and "a church for others" (Schrage 1988: 5). Jesus said we should be in the world but not of the world. New Testament ethics is not systematic. Wolfgang Schrage says we should use the term "ethics" in quotation marks. The same is true or concepts such as:

1) formal ethics,
2) situational ethics
3) personal ethics
4) social ethics
   and so on. (Schrage 1988:5).

In the New Testament ethics, very little is reflected on the problems of Christology, eschatology, ecclesiology but more is written on conduct of Christians. Schrage says;

> "It is true that the decisions recorded in the New Testament are predetermined to some degree by contemporary patterns of thought and action, value and goals. They are also shaped by many forces outside the community. Responsibility must be divided amongst various factors: religion, cultural and intellectual as well as economic, political and social." (Schrage 1988:7)

New Testament ethics share one primary common feature; their theological and Christological foundation. Its criterion and basis is God's saving act in Jesus Christ. God does everything for him. Love must be the motivating factor. We should love God supremely above all others.

The New Testament ethics is love for one another and work for the poor. Love for your enemies and praying for those who do not love you. Christianity requires that we should not do the ordinary, but above the normal and the usual. It is no question to love your friend we must love our enemy and those that persecute us. Then we will be fulfilling the golden rule, "therefore all things whatsoever ye would that men should do to you, do ye even so to them: for this is the law and the prophets" (Revelation 7:12).

2.10.1 Jesus' Eschatological Ethics

Jesus' Eschatological ethics is centered on the message of the imminent coming of the kingdom of God. We will discuss the kingdom issue as we go down. We should know whether it has come or is still coming?

2.10.2 Eschatology and Ethics

The kingdom was Jesus' theme while on earth and nothing was as good as the coming of that kingdom. Jesus in prayer said: "Thy kingdom come" (Matt. 6). To the disciples He said, "go ye therefore and preach the gospel (Matt. 28). To us He said "and this gospel of the kingdom shall be preached in all the world for a witness unto all nations and then shall the end come." (Matt. 24:14).

2.10.3 The Meaning of God's Kingdom

The Jews were expecting the establishment of David's kingdom and to be freed from oppression, yet Jesus' kingdom is not meant for the Jews alone, Jesus' kingdom is for the whole world, and according to Revelation it will start in heaven and then come down (Rev 21).

Jesus' sermons drew on this eschatological hope. For God's kingdom to come on the rebellious cosmos. Wolfgang Schrage says:

> "The Jews looked for the historical eschaton, and for Jesus, God's kingdom was not limited to the Jews and Jerusalem, but to all who will believe in Him and the Father. God's kingdom is not limited to specifics, timetable, political nationalism etc. God's kingdom is future and yet present. It has began to those who accept Jesus, and its final end is future" (Schrage 1988: 8).

The parable of the mustard seed is about the present and future. The beginning and the end cannot be separated. Jesus brought the kingdom of God all alone and He called twelve disciples and today the whole world knows about Jesus. Small seed, big shrub, (we as the disciples of Jesus are also to proclaim the kingdom and heal. We share secondarily in mediating the presence and reality of the kingdom of God". (Schrage 1988:21).

God's kingdom is brought without human help. The seed growing secretly in Mark 4:26ff. This is interpreted as the radical exclusion of all human activity. Preachers are called to preach the good news, and the results of people getting converted are the works of the Lord and the Holy Spirit. The coming God's kingdom is brought about by His alone. We must conform to the coming of the kingdom, even in what we do. "We can and must live it and extend it" (Schrage 1988:22).

We are held hostage by sin and Jesus brought the kingdom by setting us free, i.e. the blind to see, the demoniac freed, the lost to be found, the rejected by society brought back to society, the crippled made well and so on. Jesus first brought salvation to mankind before the judgment. The promise of unconditional salvation in the beatitudes brought hope to the poor, the despised, those who are mourning and those in need.

God does not operate like humans i.e. the laborers in the vineyard (Matt 20:1) they all got the same pay regardless of number of hours worked. The prodigal son had wasted all his inheritance and when he came home he was not only accepted but a great feast is given to his reception (Luke 15). God is merciful towards sinners. Jesus' ethics presupposed both the dawning kingdom of God with its gift of salvation and the assurance and expectation of its complete realization.

2.10.4 The Relationship between Eschatology and Ethics

Jesus' eschatology and his ethics cannot be separated from each other. The two work together. Some will talk of realized eschatology and the coming eschatology by their ethics, they are the same and it calls people to repentance and to accept Jesus as the savior of mankind. The end was always at hand for Jesus.

It is not all exegetes who think that Jesus' ethics is grounded in his eschatology. Some believe that the two have no relationship. "The unity of eschatology and ethics is brought in the person of Jesus, who shows the way in both" (Schrage 1988:25).

There are passages where we find a direct relationship between eschatology and ethics, e.g. (Luke 12:58, 59). We need to be ready at all times, so that we can be saved at the end. Those who will not be ready will not be saved at the end. Everything done and left undone has inescapable consequences for evil or for good, for salvation or perdition. The reward is a free gift from God.

> "The observances of the law are preconditioned for the coming of the eschaton. The apocalyptic writers are aware that obedience to the law merely prepares humankind to receive the kingdom. (Schrage 1988:28).

Jesus' message is "repent, for the kingdom of God is at hand". The parable of the treasure in the field and the valuable pearl (Matt 13: 44 – 46). We find the definition of the relationship between eschatology and ethics and Jesus' definition. Ethics here is based on the presence of the kingdom of God. Jesus said that we shall know the truth and the truth shall set us free (John 8:32).

2.10.5 Eschatology Ethics – Neither Apocalyptic nor Sapiential

Jesus' ethics is the demand for a man who knows that the kingdom of God is coming to an end. Jesus' eschatology is the end of all civilization and its value. Jesus does not want anyone to be left out of the kingdom; all must repent and be baptized.

Jesus' ethics is not determined by apocalyptic eschatology. The time is not Jesus' problem, but that people must be ready for the kingdom now, not tomorrow because we do not know about tomorrow.

Jesus' notion of God and eschatology are inseparable. The statement that, "God made the Sabbath as a blessing for human's well – being (Mark 2:27)". (Schrage 1988:32). This is a special holiday given to mankind from the beginning of creation which the Devil has been trying to destroy earth since he left heaven. Jesus came to remind mankind that this day was meant for a blessing because the leaders made it so difficult to observe so much so that it lost its meaning and was no longer a blessing. This is what the Devil wants to see. Jesus came to redeem, He is coming to reign. The Sabbath is God's authority and the devil has been questioning that authority from heaven and he has made his own Sabbath which is Sunday.

Ethics must be based on God's law, the Ten Commandments and the Bible. People teach their own will so Jesus came to bring back God's law and to show the way. Jesus came to a world which had twisted God's will and God's ways to suit their own understanding. The Jews had lost their mission of being missionaries to the cosmos. Instead of sharing the love of God with the rest of humankind they hid it under the bushel. Jesus used wisdom in his eschatological ethics, because He came to people who thought they were wise and yet were not. Jesus came to set straight the fact that Jews closed out gentiles from the kingdom of God. God wanted Jews to make God known to the nations around them.

2.10.6 Eschatological Ethics – Conforming to God's Salvation

The story of the wicked servant (Matt 18: 23) to me reveals the Jews who needed forgiveness from God and they made it so hard for others because they themselves would not make it to the kingdom. So others must fail to make it too. That is what the Devil wants. He does not want to go to hell alone; he needs some company with him. That is why he is working hard in these last days. The Devil is a lair and murderer from the beginning (John 8: 44).

2.10.7 The Law of Love in Formal Ethics and Situation Ethics

Love is the fundamental, all encompassing attitude of all individual commandments. Anyone that loves knows God because God is love. Love cannot be given a limit. Jesus said we should forgive seventy times seven (Matt 18:21, 22).

2.10.8 Love of Neighbours and Love of God

We should love the neighbors that we see and God that we do not see. Our enemies we hate we must love them as God has loved us and even died for us. An eye for an eye will leave the whole world blind. Bitten one cheek, give the other one too, one mile take him two miles instead. Jesus came to make wrong right and right, right. That is why even the poor understand Him.

2.10.9 The Double Commandment of Love

The love for God and love for our neighbor. We cannot love God without loving others. The first four commandments are love between God and man. The last six are love between man and man. In the Ten Commandments today, it is not love for the neighbor that is giving a problem to people, but love for God especially the Sabbath that is being questioned. Jesus said, if you love me, keep my commandments. We cannot say we know Him when we fail to obey Him and not doing His will. God is love and as we follow Him we should show it by loving others who are of His creation.

We can only show that we love God by also loving others. We must love doing God's will and then love our fellow man. The law of God must be kept in full. When God presented it to Moses it was complete and it needed no addition or subtraction. God wrote the law with His own hand and Moses wrote the ceremonial law. If we are good to others we have done it to God Himself. The Devil is using mankind to fight God's law and God's law does not change as God Himself does not change, He is the same yesterday, today and forever.

When Jesus talked of the double commandment; He was summarizing the Ten Commandments, not doing away with them. There were two tables of stones which Moses came with from God. One stone contained the relationship between God and man; the other stone contained the relationship between man and man. One was a horizontal (relationship) and the other diagonal (relationship). Jesus saw no love of God without love of neighbors and enemies. How do we love God and hate that which is created in His own image. How can you love God whom you have not seen and not love man that you see every day?

2.10.10 Concret Presepts

The Eschaton according to Jesus does not render concrete human conduct unimportant; it is confronted radically with challenges. The message has corporate ethics and also personal ethics. When he called the disciples he did not allow them to seek second opinion from anyone, but act immediately as called e.g. Peter, John, Matthew, almost all the disciples were called and they followed there and then. When we hear God's word we must be carefull not to wait for either Father or Mother's opinion, but accept Him immediately lest we miss life eternal on someone's opinion. (Luke 5:27 – 28).

2.10.10.1 Fundamental Consideration

Jesus' message addressed corporate ethics and personal ethics. He covered respect for authority, obeying parents, mixing with people, healing the sick etc.

Jesus preached against divorce, oaths, vengeance, hatred, loving those who love us etc. Jesus was a man of peace, love and justice. He had come to make perfect the law of God which man had made so hard and complicated for every one.

2.10.10.2 Husband and Wife/ Marriage and Divorce

Prejudice against women, slaves, gentiles and children were rife during Jesus' time. Jesus wanted all to be treated with dignity and respect. Jesus spoke well of marriage and promoted equality of both husband and wife. Divorce and adultery is against God's law. "God created marriage as a permanent union between man and women," (Schrage 1988:98). Marriage is another of God's institutions that the Devil has been fighting since creation and today the Devil has destroyed marriage completely. There are so many broken homes and families are destroyed every day in our societies. Husband and Wife do not care about the welfare of their kids when they divorce, they think just of themselves.

2.11 Concrete Ethics

2.11.1 Individual Morality

Individual morality is different from social ethics, but the difference is not very much. This only affects an individual not the society. It is one to one, not one to many.

Paul says in (1 Cor. 12:13), "There is neither slave nor free, there is neither male nor female, for you are all one in Christ Jesus". Jesus' ethics was breaking through social rules and stereotypes. He did not like classifying people, as we like doing today. We have divided people into colour.

Every individual has the right to form his/her own moral standards, the family can also form their own, but we have a standard one from the Bible which is the ten commandment. Every person under the sun and created by God must, I repeat must obey the Ten Commandments because they were made for us and for our good. The standard for all morality must be the Ten Commandments.

2.11.2 Eschatology Frame Work in Revelation

The ethics of Revelation has to do with eschatological framework of the owner of this world and the coming of the new kingdom. This kingdom will come whether we are ready or not. The entire book of Revelation is permeated by eschatology. "We have the seer's vision of the eschatological future coming from God who alone can disclose the future and thus interpret the course of history". (Schrage 1988:332).

There are two things which must soon take place and the apocalyptic determinism. Those who read and are ready are called blessed. The unique feature of eschatology in Revelation is its expectation of Christ's presence. He is Lord and Savior, God as the one who is, and was and is to come, the Alpha and the Omega (1:8). "He is the creator and the finisher, towards those saving Lordship the whole world moves". (Schrage 1988:333).

He who spoke the first words in creation will soon speak the last words in recreation. There is hope for the apocalyptic future. We have been redeem by the blood of the Lamb. He that shall endure unto the end shall be saved (1:17). Christ is Lord of lords and King of kings, (17:14; 19:16). The ruler of the king of the earth (1:5).

We can only conquer the Devil by the blood of the Lamb and by the word of their testimony. The same goes for the keeping of God's commandment that we can only keep it with the power of the blood of the Lamb and not on our own (12:10, 11). Evil will not rule this cosmos forever, but the reign of God shall come and destroy evil. These two kingdoms cannot co – exist, just like darkness cannot be where there is light.

2.11.2.1 The Letters to the Churches

The ethics of Revelation is also found in the letters. The past is revealed by these letters and the future is also revealed by the letters. Judgment will come and God's people must come out of Babylon. Every church is encouraged to conquer, because Jesus the Lion of Judah has already conquered.

In Revelation Christology and eschatology constitute the primary elements of ethics and the Christian life.

Repentance is the most frequent of the letters. The word repentance is as central to Revelation as to the gospel. We have to know the Bible in order that we can repent and we can only know if we have read the scriptures. In order to be accepted we must acknowledge the sin to the person we have sinned against and then to God too.

2.11.2.2 Conflict with the State

In Revelation we find that, there is a conflict between the will of God and that of the state. "There is collision between the Christian faith on one hand and the Roman Empire and Emperor worship on the other" (Schrage 1988:342). In Christian ethics, worship is only due to God. Worship to any creature is blasphemy to God. To the seer, the whole earth is following and worshipping the beast (13:3,8). To worship the beast is to worship on Sunday and the Pope had power to put up kings and depose them, but in 1798, his powers were taken from him by Napoleon of France (Rev. 13). We must come out of her if we are God's people.

There is a period in history when Christians were persecuted by the Pope and the Roman Catholic Church, for refusing to worship on Sunday and for refusing to believe what they taught. Many Christians lost their lives (Rev. 13: 5 – 7).

I believe that the letters to the seven churches represent the different periods of the church from the apostles to the advent. If one studies church history and compares the periods and incidence in the churches, one will come to the same conclusion that the church has always had a conflict with the state.

The Roman Empire persecuted Christians in the name of God, millions lost their lives for Christ's sake and yet they were blaspheming the name of God by making themselves to be in the place of God and forgiving sins, God alone can forgive sins.

Schnackenburg says; "the blood of the martyrs had already flowed, and was to go on flowing" (Schnackenburg 1962:378). In life, the more you refuse people to do something, the more they want to do it. Christians were motivated by the hope of the second coming of Jesus Christ as well as the love for God.

The theology and the Ethics of Revelation are founded on the trinity, God the Father, the Son and the Holy Spirit. The nearness of the coming of the Kingdom should be proclaimed. The message of Revelation needs to be given that eschatological urgency.

The book of Revelation is the book that needs to be researched carefully in its theology, ethics and exegesis because it can be easily misunderstood and read out of context. It calls people back to the law of God and to repentance. "Blessed are those who do His Commandments, that they may have the right to the tree of life, and may enter through the gates into the city" (Revelation 22:14).

CHAPTER 3

Eschatology in Revelation

3   Introduction

The book of Revelation is about Eschatology, Berkhof says the following about the coming Jesus:

> "The prophets represent the coming of the messiah and the end of the world as coinciding, the "Last days" are days immediately preceding both the coming of the messiah and the end of the world" (Berkhof 1981:666).

Christ has already come for the first time and we are now waiting for His second coming. It is not everyone who believes in the second coming of our Lord, thus not everyone believes in Eschatology.

The book of Revelation is the last book of the Bible that is full of the eschatological events of the future age. Eschatology "calls attention to the fact that the history of the world and of the human race will finally reach its consummation" (Berkhof 1981:666). The history of the world is going towards an appointed end time, where sin will be destroyed forever and ever.

There is general eschatology, and individual eschatology. The general will happen to all when Jesus comes and the individual happens to those who will die before the parousia. We all need to be ready for the two, as individuals.

3.1   The Eschatological Expection of Revelation

The book is dealing with a short time period and the main concern of Revelation is the breaking in of God's kingdom and the godless powers will be destroyed. The author knows only a short time before the eschaton. He is encouraging every one to be ready for the eschaton.

Those who have been killed for the word of God asked about time before the final judgment (6:9 – 11). "These were the souls under the alter, who were slain for their witness for God's word. They were told to wait just a little longer until the number of their fellow servants and "brethren" who are still to be killed is complete" (Fiorenza 1985:47). The believers want to see their salvation closed and complete.

3.2   The Execution Of Judgement as the Vindication of the Christian Community

In Revelation the whole eschatological presentation culminates in judgment and salvation. All visions, all descriptions, all events lead to the beginning of the final eschatological salvation. "The goals of the whole book of apocalypses is the final judgment and the eschatological salvation" (Fiorenza 1985:47).

The book of apocalypse is the book of Great Controversy between good and evil and the final destruction of evil by God. It warns every one to repent and be ready. The final events are rough for the Christians who find their hope being tested. Their prayer is that the Lord should come very soon.

The proclamation of the gospel to all nations is the prerequisite for the end and we should not fear anything not even death. "And this gospel of the kingdom will be preached as a witness to all nations, and then the end shall come" (Matt 24:14). Eschatology and ecclesiology are in the theology of Revelation and are very closely related.

3.3   The Date or Time of Judgment

There are two fold answers to the date or time of judgment. They must wait just a "little while" while they wait for the persecutions of the Christians to be completed. The seer awaits in the immediate future which he saw in visions and He heard the promise, "I am coming soon" (22:20; 22:8; 2:16; 3:11). He is already at the door (3:20) and He will soon bring in the reward with him. We must all be watchful for Him will come like a thief (3:3; 16:15). The Lord is coming soon and we should do our part in making sure we hasten His coming. Then He who promised will not delay.

3.4   The Situation of the Community until the Final Judgement

The battle between the Kingdom of God and the kingdom of Satan will take place on earth. Jesus has overcome the

Devil on the cross. The two witnesses have been slain (the Old and the New Testament). Though Christians are killed for the witness of Jesus, they have not given up. The Devil is very angry because he knows the time is very short. Fiorenza says;

> "Just as the victory of the Lamb in death was the prerequisite for His heavenly reign, so also the victory of the Christians in death is the prerequisite for the coming of God's rule on earth (6:9)" (Fiorenza 1985:50).

The Devil has been defeated on the cross and there is no way he will ever win. When Christ rose from the dead, He gave the Devil the last blow. We who are Christ's followers are over comers if we will not give up the battle against the evil one. The Devil will not give Christians peace because he wants to confuse everyone to follow him. John says we must hold on, Jesus is coming soon.

3.5   The Composition of Revelation

The main theme of Revelation is three according to Fiorenza.

1) The establishment of the kingdom of God and Christ in judgement.
2) The imminent expectation, which knows only a short duration of time until the end.
3) The prophetic interpretation of the present situation of the Christian community. We will briefly look at these themes of Revelation.

3.5.1   The Ecclesiai Framework

The book is a formal letter to seven churches which may fit in any church situation till the end of time. It is a prophetic writing to the churches. The eschatological conclusion ends in a prologue and the vision of the new Jerusalem.

3.5.2   The Description of the Little while before the End

The little While separates the present time from the eschatological future. The final time will be the time of Antichrist, war, hunger, and death and they will be filled with cosmic catastrophes and demoniac onslaughts. The angels will be pouring the last vials of God's wrath to the wicked. The time before the end will be a time of testing and trial. It had to be shortened lest many would not make it at all. The Little while is seen as a time of witnessing for the Christians. Antichrist dominates the whole earth.

3.5.3   The Description of God's Judgement

The theme of judgment is broadly developed in the visions of the cosmic plagues and in the last visions of the new world. The whole book of Revelation reaches climax in the description of judgment and of eschatological salvation. The reader is always confronted with the end. Revelation is the end of the Bible and it talks about last things (Eschatology).

This cosmos is now in the hands of the Devil but when God shall judge, things will change and the kingdom of God will rule the world, not sin any more.

3.6   Individual Eschatology

We will not deal much with individual eschatology, but these deal with physical death which comes to every individual and it is physical, spiritual and eternal. Death of believers is called sleep because they have the hope of the resurrection in the parousia. The wicked have no hope in their death.

3.7   General Eschatology

When Jesus comes He will come for all at once. He will not come to take us one by one as some people believe, but He will come for all of us at the same time when the trumpet shall sound. The whole world will know about it, it will be the great day of the Lord.

3.7.1   The Second Coming of Christ

The coming of Christ is two fold, He came to redeem and He is coming to reign. He came as a baby and He is coming for the second time to take the saints home for one thousand years. He talked about it and the angels told the disciples about it.

3.7.2   The Second Coming a Single Event

The second coming of Christ will be a single event and all eyes shall see Him. The dead saints will be raised from their graves and the living saints will be changed to meet the Lord in the air (1 Cor. 15:48 – 58). There are those who talk about the secret rapture, but there in no scriptural proof to that effect and I do not believe in it. Jesus will come once for the saints, and the saints will be raised and the living saints will be changed immediately into new bodies.

3.8   The Manner of the Second Coming

There are many ways that have been discovered and taught of how Christ is going to come in this world, but when He shall appear the coming will be personal, visible, sudden, glorious and triumphant. All eyes shall see Him in the cloud.

3.8.1   It will be a Personal Coming

Jesus Christ will come in person and we have a lot of assurance from the Bible. "This Jesus, who was received up from you into heaven, shall so come in like manner as ye beheld Him going into heaven". Acts 1:11; 3:20,21; Matt. 24:44; 1 Cor. 15:22; Phil 3:20; Col 3:4; 1 Thess 2:19; 3:13; 4:15 – 17; 11 Tim 4:8; Tit 2:13; Heb 9:28;. He will not send an angel to come or anyone, but He will come the same way He was seen going up into heaven.

3.8.2   It will be a Physical Coming

The Lord's return will be a physical one not a spiritual one. There are verses to support this belief. Act 1:11; 3:20 – 21; Heb 9:28; Rev 1:7. he will return to earth in the body. He has not yet come, but when He does, this world will be left desolate and the Devil will be left alone with no one to deceive. He will come with the Angels to take us to heaven.

3.8.3   It will be a Visible Coming

The coming of the Lord will be physical and visible. Jesus is a man of His word and He would not want to disappoint His followers. He said to the disciples that He is going to prepare a place so that where He is, His disciples also may be. If it was not so He would have told them. He is coming back again.

When Christ shall appear, He will be visible. There are verses from the Bible to support this, Matt 24:30; Tit 2:13; Heb 9:28; Rev 1:7. he will come to take us home to the Father and He will not want anyone to usher us in. he will want to do it Himself.

3.8.4   It will be a Sudden Coming

The Bible talks of signs of His coming, but on the same note it talks of Christ's sudden coming and He will come like a thief, when He is least expected. That is why His followers are urged to be ready at all times. Berkhof says, "The coming will be sudden, will be rather unexpected, and will take people by surprise" (Berkhof 1981:706). (Matt 24: 37 – 44); 25: 1 – 12; 1 Thess 5:23; Rev 3:3; 16:15)

When Jesus Christ came for the first time, He took many by surprise and yet many signs were told of His coming. The mission of John the Baptist was long foretold, but many with scriptures in their hands and studying daily did not recognize all these things when they came to fulfillment. Followers of Christ should not be found sleeping with the

Bibles in their hands when Jesus comes. The story of the ten virgins should be taken seriously.

> "The Bible intimates that the measure of the surprise at the second coming of Christ will be in an inverse ratio to the measure of their watchfulness" (Berkhof 1981:706).

3.8.5   It will be a Glorious and Triumphant Coming

When He comes, He will be coming in glory and He will overcome as He has already overcome. Berkhof says the second coming though personal, physical and visible, will yet be very different from His first coming. "He will not return in the body of His humiliation, but in a glorified body and royal apparel, Heb 9:28" (Berkhof 1981:706)

He will come as King of kings and Lord of lords. He will over power all the forces of evil and will put all His enemies under His feet. 1 Cor 15:25; Rev 19:11 – 16; 1981:706. God has been very patient with us sinners and He wants all to be saved into the kingdom. God is love and cannot force any one to accept Him as his personal savior. The Devil was given all kinds of opportunities to repent, but he refused all of them.

3.9   The Purpose of the Second Coming

Our Lord will return at the end of the age to introduce the future age and the eternal state of things. Berkhof says, He will do it by completing two mighty events namely, "the resurrection of the dead and the final judgment" (Berkhof 1981:708). Rev 20:11 – 15; 22:12.

The scripture said the end of the world, the day of the Lord, the physical resurrection of the dead, and the final judgment shall mark the second coming of Christ when all the evil forces destroyed. Rev 20:14. the Lord will come to fulfill the hope of his people.

3.10 The Final State of Eschatological Judgement

The last judgment will lead on too the final state of he righteous and the evil ones. All must come to an end somehow and cannot continue. The righteous will not continue suffering forever, while the evil of the Devil continues to enjoy forever. Sin must come to an end while good must begin to rule. The going out of the Devil's reign of terror, should bring in the reign of the king of kings and the Lord of lords.

3.10.1 The Final State of the Wicked

God has always been open about the state of the wicked and the state of the righteous and it is full all over the Bible about the state of both groups and a warning has been issued and all of us have the power to choose life or death. There are three points to be considered for the final state of the wicked:

3.10.1.1 The Place to which the Wicked are Consigned

The Bible talks about the hell of fire where the wicked will burn for ever and ever. But modern theology does not want to believe in perpetual burning. It talks about ending of the punishment of all sinners. The scripture speaks of those excluded from heaven as being "outside" and as being "cast into hell".

Luke 16: 19 – 31, this is the story of the rich man and Lazarus, who both died. Lazarus went to heaven, the rich man went to hell. The rich man who enjoyed on earth was now suffering in hell while Lazarus who suffered on earth is now enjoying in heaven. The punishment of the wicked will be eternal (Without reverse). The wicked will be doomed forever and ever.

3.10.1.2 The State in which they will Continue Their Existence

According to Berkhof, there are four things that we are sure of about the punishment of the wicked:

1) A total absence of the favor of God.
2) An endless disturbance of life as a result of the favor of God.
3) Positive pains and suffering in body and soul, and
4) Such subjective punishment as pangs of conscience, anguish, despair, weeping and gnashing teeth (Matt 8:12; 13:50; Rev 14:10; 21:8) 1981:736.

There shall be fire from heaven and many will wish they had listened to the voice of God than the Devil. The state of the Devil will not be a good one. We need to accept Jesus as our personal savior now before it's too late.

3.10.1.3   The Duration of Their Punishment

The Bible talks of everlasting and eternal death and punishment. Some talk of burning for ever and ever, but I believe from past prophecies and evidence where God talks of destroying the cities of Sodom and Gomorrah for ever or eternally and He meant that they shall never exist and it is true, they have never existed to this day. I believe that when God talks of eternal fire, He means when the wicked are destroyed, they will never ever exist again. So sin and sinners will be destroyed forever, never to be seen or heard again. The fire will stop, but the damage will never be reversed. It will be forever and ever more.

The term for the punishment of the wicked is the same as the one used for the righteous. People have no problem with everlasting bliss, but cannot accept everlasting fire. Anyway some questions will be answered by Jesus when we get to heaven, Mark 9: 43.

3.10.2   The Final State of the Righteous

3.10.2.1   The New Creation

After a thousand years is over God will destroy the sinners and the world and He will create the new heaven and the new earth. There will be regeneration and restoration of all things. Heb 12:27. God will make all things new and evil will never reign again and we will eat from the tree of life and drink the water of life forever and ever. Rev 21: 1 – 6).

3.10.2.2 The Eternal Abode of the Rightious

Heaven is a place and it is not here on earth or a person. It is a real place where God dwells and wants His people to be. Jesus said He was going to prepare a place for His followers. There are mansions where He has gone, (John 4:1). The righteous will not only inherit the heavens, but also the earth. The believers are said to be within the gate and unbelievers are without the walls of the city.

3.10.2.3 The Nature of Their Reward

The reward is eternal life, which is not only endless, but life in all its fullness. The present and past will be gone for good. (Matt 25:46; Rom 2:7). God Himself will be there to make life real fulfilling. (Rev 21:3). The saints will see Jesus face to face. Their joy will be perfect and full. We have not seen nor heard what God has prepared for his children. It is beyond dreams and imagination. Nothing is like unto it on earth.

Conclusion

Eschatology as discussed, is the doctrine of the last things or last day events and revelation. The last book of the Bible closes with the end of this world's history which is coming fast to its close. It is an open book as compared to Daniel's book which was a closed book that was to be opened later. We are to study this book carefully or else we are going to miss out on the kingdom of God and the blessings He has reserved for those who will follow him. There is no one who would like to miss out on such a wonderful experience which will never ever be repeated.

CHAPTER 4

The Role of the Spirit in Revelation

In the book of Revelation, the Holy Spirit is mentioned many times. We are going to look at the verses very closely, in order to understand more about the Spirit and even identify its role. The Holy Spirit played a great role in the book of Revelation and in the New Testament. It is through the Spirit that John received the vision as we see it in Revelation today.

Bauckam says the following concerning the Spirit:

> "References to the Spirit of God in Apocalypse can be divided in three categories : four occurrences of the phrases 'in the Spirit'(1:10;4:2;17:3;21:10); ten other references to the Spirit (2:7;11,17,29;3:6,13,2 2;14:13;19:10;22:17). (Bauckam 1993:150).

We are going to look at the above verses very carefully in the paragraphs that are going to follow. We need to understand the role of the Spirit very much in order to understand the book of Revelation.

4   The Spirit of Vision

The spirit of vision is found in the following verses (Rev. 1:10; 4:2; 17:3; 21;10). John was the one who saw the visions while in the Isle of Patmos. We will also try to consider each one of them according to its merit. Bauckham says:

> "In every Christian literature the phrase commonly means 'in the spirit's control' with various connotations. Frequently it denotes temporary experience of the spirit's power in prophetic speech or revelation, without specifying any particular mode of Spirit's operation". (Bauckham 1993:150).

John received the visions while he was in the spirit but it was not only one time, but several times. Each time John received the vision he recorded it and sometimes even mentioned the day which he received the vision. All these took place while he was in the island of Patmos where he was the prisoner for the word of God. God brought the whole history of the world to his view.

4.1   The Spirit in the Vision of the Glorified Christ

John says; "I was in the Spirit on the Lord's Day, and heard behind me great voices, as of a trumpet" (Rev 1:10). John saw the vision of a glorified Christ on the Lord's Day. In this first vision, John has also given us the day in which he saw the vision. Which one is the Lord's Day?

Schrage's interpretation of the Lord's Day is that it refers to Sunday and many other scholars believe that Sunday is the Lord's Day. However, I have a different opinion on this and will draw the support from the Bible. The Lord's Day is Sabbath which is the seventh day of the week as we start counting from Sunday as the first day. In the book of Genesis when God was creating the world, he called the days as the first day, the second day, the third day, the fourth day, the fifth day, the sixth day and then the seventh day which is also called the Sabbath of the Lord. (Genesis 1:1-13).

The Bible clearly lays down the seventh day as "the Sabbath" and should be set aside as a day holy and sanctified by God, this was laid down in the Decalogue (Exodus 20:8-11). The fourth commandment (Exodus 20:8-11) is based at the fact that God Himself rested (literally, ceased) from His creative labour on the seventh "day" of the creation week. (Gen 2:2). The principle still applies today; the day is still blessed even today.

The Sabbath was a gift from God (Cf Exodus 16:29). He created it in commemoration of his creative work and His creatures can acknowledge His authority as the creator of anything that exists. God had also a humanitarian purpose for this day in which slaves were shown mercy by being allowed a regular rest from all their labour (Deut 5:14ff). "The Sabbath is celebrated to remember God as the creator of all living creatures" (the new concise Bible dictionary).

In the New Testament, Jesus repeats the claim of the Sabbath as a very special day. He also claims it to be His Day. Mark 2:27, 28 read: "…. The Sabbath was made for man and not man for Sabbath: therefore the Son of man is Lord also of the Sabbath". Throughout the Bible, God refers to the Sabbath as His Sabbaths" (Ex. 31:13; Exek 20:12,20; 44:24; Rom 9:29; James 5:4). Jesus never came to change any law, He only came to fulfill it and make it possible for His followers to keep it.

There is no scripture text that shows that the sanctity as instituted on the Sabbath by God has been transferred to the first day of the week. Jesus himself kept the Sabbath even unto His death. So John was in the Spirit on the Lord's Day which is the Sabbath. Further verses on the Lord's day can be found in (Matt 12:8; Luke 6:5; Acts 5:31; Romans 10:9, 1 Col 1:9; 1 Cor 8:6, 12:3; Eph 4:5 and Psalms 118:24). The Lord's day in Revelation is a theological issue which needs to be studied very well before the son of man comes again because the Devil has laid a trap on that verse and many are going to be lost if we are not careful, and reading the scriptures.

Bacchiocchi when he talks about the relevance of the Sabbath says:

> "The Sabbath is relevant for the modern persons because it nourishes such a three – dimensional faith. The themes of the Sabbath, ... encompass creation, redemption and final restoration; the past, the present and the future; man, nature and God... the Sabbath provides modern believers with a basis for a Sabbath provides modern believers with a basis for a cosmic faith: a faith that reaches out to the past, present and future realities" (Bacchiocchi 1980:19).

God is a particular God and He does not leave man to walk in darkness without telling him what he is and how he should be worshipped. It was not a mistake that God did not give days their names but He wanted to name only one day because he wanted man to remember that day on a weekly basis in order to honour Him who created the heavens and the earth in six days and rested on the Seventh day which is the Sabbath of the Lord.

4.1.1   The Spirit in the Vision of Throne of God in Heaven

In Revelation 4:2 John says "and immediately I was in the Spirit and behold, a throne was set in heaven, and one sat on the throne". In the vision John saw the elders, the four living creatures, and the united worship of God. He saw what takes place in the throne room of God the Almighty who is the only one worthy to be worshipped and be praised.

John in a vision saw the throne room of God which is the hope of this hopeless world. It is the same throne room which God planned the foundations of this world and all the creatures created. When John saw it, God was showing him that he was going to recreate this world anew. John saw the destruction of this world and the new city coming down from heaven. John was filled with hope and he wrote this good news so that we can also be filled with hope that comes to us from the throne of God.

The throne of God brings us Biblical hope, which Paul declares, "May the God of hope fill you with all joy and peace in believing, so that by the power of the Holy Spirit you may abound in hope" (Rom. 15:13). Bacchiocchi says, "Hope is derived from God's provision of salvation through Jesus Christ. .... By accepting Christ's provision of salvation the believer is "born anew to a living hope" (1 Pet 1:3) of eternal life and fellowship with God (Rev 21:3) "(Bacchiocchi 1986:24).

4.1.2   The Spirit in the Vision of the Mystic Babylon

The term mystic Babylon has a dual meaning in that the first word means mystry and the second one means confusion (Babylon). John saw the mixture of paganism and religion in one religious group and he saw the confusion and he called it the mystical Babylon. The woman represents the church, but this church is sitting on top of a scarlet beast which is full of blasphemy. The term blasphemy means making yourself to be in the place of God a representative of God on earth, there is only one God the Holy Spirit. That is the one Christ promised he will send to come and reveal more about himself, not a human being in a form of a harlot or a church that is not faithful.

In Revelation 17:3 we read "So he carried me away in the Spirit into the wilderness and I saw a woman sitting upon a scarlet beast which was full of names of blasphemy, having seven heads and ten horns". In this vision John sees a lot of symbols. The woman is a church and the beast may represent a government which associates itself with the church. The symbolism of Revelation needs to be looked at very closely through Bible study before interpretation can be given.

The mystical Babylon is a mixture of Church and state. This power is neither religious nor pagen, but confusion called mystical Babylon. The woman seen is a harlot which means a woman of many husbands, a church of many followed and wondered after the beast and they said no one is like unto the beast. We need to be very careful about what we follow and believe because it is dangerous to just follow anything in this day and age. Many false prophets will come, Jesus warned his disciples and us too. The harlot is an unfaithful woman or unfaithful church.

4.1.3   The Spirit in the Vision of the Bride, the Lamb's Wife

In this vision of Revelation 21:10, John says "And He carried me away in the Spirit to a great and high mountain, and showed me that great city, the holy Jerusalem descending out of heaven from God". John was shown in vision the new Jerusalem, the bride, the Lamb's wife, prepared for marriage with the Lamb. This is the true church made new, the right bride for the Lamb.

In the book of Ephesians 5: 20 – 30, Paul talks to the church about wives and husbands submitting to each other and the wife is likened to the church while the husband is likened to Christ. The church is the wife of the Lamb, Jesus Christ. He even died for the church on the cross. Husbands must love their wives unto death. John goes on to describe the beauty and the size of the city. The name Jerusalem means the city of peace. There will be peace inn that city and the saints will live for ever and ever. Today we have so many churches it is hard to find the right one, without the guidance of the Holy Spirit.

4.2   The Spirit Of Prophecy

God could no longer speak to and phase to phase after sin entered the world and he decided to use prophets. "Surely the Lord God will do nothing; He reveals His secret unto His servants the prophets" (Amos 3:7). There is a need for a prophetic gift today. Jemison says, "Communication to the prophets generally came in the form of visions or dreams. "If there be a prophet among you, I the Lord will make Myself known unto him in a vision, and will speak unto him in a dream" (Numbers 12: 6). God opened to His chosen men scenes of the past, present and future and He directed them to speak, write or retain their revelations as the occasion demanded" (Jemison 1955: 23 -24).

According to Mrs. White,

> "The gift of prophecy was manifested in the church during the Jewish dispensation. It disappeared for a few centauries on account of the corrupt state of the church. Towards the close of that dispensation, it reappeared to usher in the messiah" {White 1858:5).

When Jesus left this world He promised to send his followers a comforter who would come and show them what to do and reveal the father and the future, which is the Holy Spirit. It is the Holy Spirit that gives the Christians the courage and the power to stand firm even when they are facing death.

The gift of prophecy and the Spirit are almost the same. The Bible is the book of prophecy. It tells about salvation and future events. God in scripture says that there is nothing He will do without telling His servants, the prophets who must in turn tell it to the rest of the world. The Gift and the Spirit of prophecy will be discussed later on.

4.2.1   The Spirit to the Churches of Asia Minor

When Christ said a word of reproof or commendation to each church, He concluded by saying: "He that hath an ear, let him hear what the Spirit says unto the churches …" Revelation 2:7, 11, 29. In every verse there were other comments added e.g. the second death shall not hurt the overcomer, the overcomer shall eat from the tree of life etc.

The Spirit is encouraging the followers to be overcomers so that they may have their names written in the book of life. The role of the Spirit is to give warning and to encourage people through the struggle with sin. The churches were going through tough times and they needed rebuke and commendation at the same time. The Spirit through John prepared the churches to go through it all and the same message applies to us today who are going to be persecuted for the word of God.

4.2.2   What the Spirit says to the Churches

To the three last churches of Sardis, Philadelphia and Laodicea, Christ changed the approach and said "He that has an ear, let him hear what the Spirit saith unto the churches" (3:6, 13 and 22). To the previous churches He added a blessing which is not pronounced to these three churches. We are to read carefully the letters to the churches so that we can find what is referred to us in the letters to the seven churches.

The" hearing" was mentioned with each church's experience which shows the importance of hearing what the Spirit says to the churches. The Spirit did not talk to the churches in Asia Minor only, but to modern churches as well. Revelation is preparing us for the events of the tribulation that Christians are going to go through and how God is going to intervene in the process. We should hold fast that which we have so that no one should snatch it from our hand.

4.2.3 The Blessedness of the Saintly Dead

The saints that are dead are called blessed because their lives are hidden in Jesus and when He shall appear they will be like Him. They will never see death again after the resurrection. They will live forever and ever. That is why they are blessed. John says, "And I heard a voice from heaven saying unto me, write, blessed are the dead which die in the Lord from hence forth: Yes saith the Spirit, that they may rest from their labours; and their works do follow them"(14:13). God pronounces a blessing to those who die in the Lord.

It is a blessing to die in the Lord because this means resting from labor and when Jesus shall come they will be raised to life eternal. There are seven apocalyptic beatitudes in Revelation,

"Like the sermon on the Mount, the Revelation breathes the benediction of heaven. Note these beatitudes:

"Blessed is he that readeth, and they that hear" 1:3.

"Blessed are the dead who die in the Lord" 14:13.

"Blessed is he that watcheth and keepeth his garments" 16:15.

"Blessed are they which are called unto the Marriage upper" 19:9.

"Blessed and holy is he that hath part in the first resurrection" 20:6.

"Blessed is he that keepeth the saying of the prophecy of this book" 22:7.

"Blessed are they that do His commandments "or" those who wash their robes" (r.s.v.) 22:14" (Anderson 1953: 6 – 7).

In this world of sin it is not a beautiful thing to be a saint because there are many hardships that the devil brings to us to try to win to his side and he is working hard to make life real hard for the followers of Christ. It may not be a blessing to be a Christian now but it will be a blessing to die on the Lord's side because when Jesus comes He will come with a reward of life eternal. That will be more than any blessing given to mankind.

4.2.4   Spirit of Prophecy

The angel brought the testimony of Jesus, "for the testimony of Jesus is the Spirit of prophecy" (19:10). The followers of Jesus Christ should spend a lot of time in studying the Spirit of prophecy in order to understand the scriptures well. In climax of prophecy we read, "Thus the Spirit of prophecy speaks through the Christian prophets bringing the word of the exalted Christ to His people on earth, and directing the prayers of the churches to their heavenly Lord....the Spirit of prophecy" (Bauckham 1993:160).

According to Larry Wilson "The remnant are identified in Revelation as keeping the commandments of God and having the Testimony of Jesus" (Rev 12:17). "In Revelation we learn that the Testimony of Jesus is the Spirit of prophecy" (Wilson 1992:305). Satan has obscured the law of God and he can counterfeit the Spirit of prophecy. So that if we are not careful we may not know which one is the true one or the false one. We need to study the Bible on our own and read Revelation very prayerfully.

The "gift of prophecy" or "the Spirit of prophecy" is "the gift of knowing the unknown" (Wilson 1992:305). According to Webster, prophecy is a "a prediction made under divine influence and direction, or a discourse made or delivered by a prophet under divine direction" (Webster dictionary 1992 edition). The Bible talks of the gift of the Spirit and they are many of them e.g. tongues, teaching, hospitality, Preaching, Prophecy etc. The Spirit of prophecy is given to the church in the last days and the true church must keep the commandments of God and must be having the testimony of Jesus and the testimony of Jesus is the Spirit of Prophecy.

There are two kinds of prophets, True and False. Therefore Christians should look at the Biblical tests of a true prophet of God in order to distinguish between the true prophets and the false one. Jamison has the following tests from the Bible.

Test 1. "To the law and to the testimony: if they speak not according to this word, it is because there is no light in them" (Isaiah 8:20) (Jemison 1955:100).

Test 2. "Wherefore by their fruits ye shall know them" Matt 7:20. (Jemison 1955:104)

Test 3. "When the word of the prophet shall come to pass, then shall the prophet be known that the Lord hath truly sent him" (Jeremiah 28:9).

Test 4. "Every Spirit that confesseth that Jesus is come in the flesh is of God". 1 John 4:2. There are other additional evidence which is the physical manifestations of a prophet, timeless, the certainty and the fearless, high spiritual plane, practical nature. God has made plans and told us that no one should be lost when the Bible and the prophets are there.

4.2.4.1 By Their Fruits you Shall Know Them

Jesus said that the false prophets shall be identified by their fruits, (Matt 7: 15 – 20). He went on to say that not every one who says Lord will enter into the kingdom of heaven, only those who do the will of my Father in heaven (Matt 7: 21 – 23). The Devil is performing a lot of miracles through his angels and many people think it is God's power. The will of God must be done first, before miracles can be performed.

Satan has power to do wonders and many of his angels are out to deceive many. Many revivals are taking place where miracles of healing are being done but people are not warned about the coming of Jesus Christ that must take place soon. They should speak according to the law and to the testimony. If they refuse the law of God, then we should not believe them at all.

4.2.4.2   Many Prophets will come in Jesus' Name

Christians must be very careful about prophets because many will claim the power of God and even say Christ has come. We are told that we should not believe them (Matt 24: 23 – 25). Satan has made people believe that the dead go to heaven or hell when they die. "He will stage some series of demonstrations that will capture the attention of the world" (Larry 1992:312). He will even make fire to come down from heaven. The beast will make many wonders, but we are told to come out of her, if we are God's people. We should not follow the majority in their wrong.

4.2.4.3   To the Law and the Testimony

A true prophet must speak according, "…. to the law and the testimony of God. If they do not speak according to this word, they have no light in them" (Isaiah 8: 19, 20). The words of the prophets should agree with the scripture and the law of God. If they do not agree with the scripture and the law of God. If they do not agree then they should not be accepted as messengers from God. They must be tested at all times, make no mistakes about it. Blessed is he that readeth the words found in this book.

Prophets who lead people to rebel against God's commandments cannot have the true gift of prophecy. In Revelation, the remnant are not only identified as having the gift of prophecy, but they "obey the commandments of God" (Wilson 1992:312). (John 14:28). They also have the testimony of Jesus. Study the Bible and find out which one is the remnant church. My definition for the remnant is, the little that remains when the rest has gone out. This is the original church, which God started in Genesis. It has remained with the truth of the Bible while others have thrown the truth through the windows of their Churches.

When Christians claim to know God they must do His will and keep His commandments. John says; the man who says "I know Him", but does not do what He commands is a liar, and the truth is not in him. But if anyone obeys His word God's love is truly made complete in him. This is how we know we are in Him: "Whoever claims to live in Him must walk as Jesus did" (1 John 2: 4 – 5).

Many people, the world over have no problem with the law as such, but have a problem with the Sabbath commandment in the Decalogue. The law is not a law without the Sabbath. The Devil fights the Sabbath because he knows he is teaching people to fight the authority of the creator. The Sabbath has to do with the creator. It was given to man before sin came into the world; it was given to man before there were people called Jews. The Sabbath has to do with commemorating God's creative power, remembering Him as the creator of the world and everything that exists. We must love God supremely that we will have no problem with

His law in totality. Narrow is the road that leads to eternal life and wide is the road that leads to destruction and many are they that go in it.

4.2.4.4 Every Spirit should be tried to see if it is from God

In 1 John 4:1 – 6 we find the following, "Beloved believe not every spirit, but try the spirit whether they are from God; because many false prophets are gone out into the world" (4.1). We should know the Spirit of God in order to know that which is not from God. Every Spirit that confesses that Jesus Christ is come in the flesh is of God (4:2).

The person with the gift of prophecy must edify or strengthen the believers. The message of a true prophet should bring people to repentance. In (1 Cor 14:3, 23, 25), we learn that prophecy edifies and it strengthens the believer and encourages and comforts. Christians need more of God's prophecy. Then if it does not edify and comfort it is not from God, but from the Devil.

4.2.4.5 The Condition of a Prophet when in Vision

When the prophet is in vision, he/she remains unconscious of the surroundings in which they are, their gaze and motions are transfixed. They do not do all the normal activities that they usually do when they are not in vision, sometimes they do not even breath, (Daniel 10: 8, 9). Modern day prophets kick around and shout hallelujahs and speak in tongues, they practice so many gifts at the same time and all of them have the same gifts and the Bible talks of each having a different gift of the Spirit. We should be careful of the Devil's counterfeits.

Revelation predicts that the gift of prophecy will be an identifying mark of the obedient remnant as well as the keeping of the commandment of God including the seventh – day Sabbath of the week. Man cannot be trusted with divine things, (Matt 15:7 – 9).

4.2.5   The Universal Invitation

The Spirit and the bride are inviting every one to come and hear the prophecy of the book of Revelation. The book is full of promises, (Rev 22:17 – 20). The role to which Revelation calls all Christians, is that of being witnesses of Jesus, remaining faithful in word and deed to the one true God and His righteousness. It won't be long He is coming back again.

There are prophecies addressed to the churches and on the other hand, the churches' prophetic witness to the world. Both are the witness of Jesus and the word of God. "They both carry God's truth and His righteousness. They are both inspired by the divine Spirit as God's power in the world. They both concern the establishment of God's kingdom in the world" (Bauckham 1993:121).

4.3   The Seven Spirit

The seven Spirit are the third and last category in the references to the Spirit in Revelation. We have discussed previously that seven is a number of completeness or a number of perfection. It is a number of God. The seven candle sticks and stands, the seventh day of the week, the seven churches, seven angels etc.

These are the seven lamps of fire burning before the throne and they are the Spirit of God. John was trying to describe the throne of God that he saw in a vision. The same ministering Spirits are the ones that have worked hand in hand with the holy Spirit to make sure the message reaches John and it should also reach some of us in due course. The Spirit has a very great role to play in the eschatological ethics of Revelation and beyond.

4.3.1   The Seven Spirits before the Throne

John is delighted to write to the seven churches by the one who is and who was and who is to come. The message also comes from the seven Spirits which are before the throne (1:4). The seven Spirits are sometimes referred to as angels around the throne or just as Spirits. The throne is in complete security because, there are seven Spirits and the number is a complete and perfect one.

The salutation explains about Jesus Christ and how He is the faithful witness. He is the first fruits of the dead and He is the Prince of the kings of the earth. He loved us and washed our sins by His own blood. He is the beginning and the end. Revelation is a book about Christ and His love for mankind. It is the book about the redemption of mankind.

4.3.2   The Message to Sardis

The message comes from Him that has the seven Spirits of God, and has the seven stars. The number seven is now doubled which may mean more power of he truthfulness of God. Everywhere in Revelation, one reads about Christ. That is why others call it the Revelation of Jesus Christ.

The Spirit was sending the word of warning to Sardis because it has not been doing well Spiritually. Sardis was told to be watchful and strengthen in things which remain. Those things should not be left to die. Watch out I will come as a thief.

4.3.3   The Seven Lamps which are the Seven Spirits

The seven Spirits of God are now identified with the seven lamps of the fire burning. The Holy Spirit is sometimes likened to a fire. These are mysteries of divine things of God. He repeats the same thing in different ways in order to make sure that those who receive the message may not be mistaken, i.e. "I am the Alpha and the Omega, the beginning and the end." He repeats the same message in order to put emphasis. God cannot be mistaken because He will repeat the same information more times in order to make sure it is heard.

These seven spirits are very closely associated with the lamb, who is said to have "seven horns and seven eyes, which are the seven Spirits of God sent out into all the earth" (Rev 4:5). As already pointed out, the number seven goes on and on and describes the completeness of that which it is explained.

4.3.4   The Seven Horns and Eyes

The lamb that was slain was seen in the throne, it had seven horns and seven eyes which are referred to as the seven Spirits. This may represent the heavenly sanctuary, because we see the; lamb that was slain in the throne, which is a sign of sacrifice in heaven. Christ is the lamb that was slain from the foundation of the world.

The seven horns, the seven eyes are said to be the seven Spirits of God which are sent out throughout the world. God's eyes range throughout the world to see what is going on and nothing passes His eyes without notice, Nothing is too small for God and nothing is too big for Him to see. He sees them all, but He will not be rushed to bring everything to eschatological ending.

The seven horns represent the Divine power of God and Christ against the four horns of the beast, which will be rendered powerless when Christ shall come. These Spirits are sent out throughout the earth to make sure that victory is effective through out the world. The lamb has defeated the Devil on the cross and when He rose from the grave. He is going to destroy him for ever when he comes the second time. The Devil was defeated in Heaven and He was throne down on earth and He is going to be defeated in his own territory once and for all.

Conclusion

There are so many questions that need great research on this topic of the Spirit in Revelation. I will only pick those that worry me most and conclude them with the Bible and personal opinions,

1) The Lord's day
2) The testimony of Jesus
3) The Spirit of prophecy
4) The remnant church.

1   The Lord's Day

The Lord's Day is bringing problems to people all over the world, many believed that the Lord's day is Sunday. It has been translated that John was in the Spirit on Sunday which is the Lord's Day. Sunday has been traditionally viewed by many Christians as the day of which Christ is Lord and which is consecrated to Him. Millions of people have not heard this statement being challenged and the Devil has made people very comfortable with Sunday as the Lord's Day, but it is not.

From Genesis, through Exodus, Leviticus, Numbers, and Deuteronomy and in the New Testament, the Lord's Day is the Sabbath. (Genesis 2:1 – 4; Ex 20:8 – 11; Heb 4:4; Mark 2:27 – 28; Luke 4:16; Isaiah 58:1 – 13 etc.). There is no where told that whoever takes out from the prophecy, his name will be taken out from the book of life. There should be no addition and no subtraction from the word of God.

The Jews had made the Sabbath to be such a burden to people and so Christ came to show His followers how to observe it. He said it was a day of joy, worship, healing and more so, it was made for the good man (Mark 2:27 – 28). The Sabbath has to do with man's redemption. Dr. Bacchiocchi says the Sabbath is a window of eternity: "The Sabbath affords the means of recapturing some measure of Edenic delight. It offers the opportunity to look at the world through the window of eternity ... Isaiah calls the Sabbath "a delight," and a day to "take delight in the Lord" (58:13 – 14). (Bacchiocchi 1980:74).

2   The Testimony of Jesus

This is the testimony that Jesus is the son of God and He was with God in the beginning as the word. He came to this world a baby and He grew up, was baptized by John in the Jordan river. He preached the good news of salvation. He was crucified on the cross and on the third day He rose from the grave. He did that to afford all believers before the cross and after the cross to have eternal life if they believe in Him then and if the present ones will believe in Him now.

Forty days after His resurrection, He was translated into heaven. Before He was translated He promised the out pouring of the Holy Spirit on the disciples and all those who will believe and be baptized in His name. the other promise was that He will come and take home all who believe, the dead and the living together. This is the testimony of Jesus, to know that the Sabbath is a delight, the law of God is holy and good and to know that God does not change. He is the same yesterday, today and forever.

3   The Spirit of Prophecy

The testimony of Jesus is the Spirit of prophecy. The Spirit of prophecy is one of the Spiritual gifts that will be seen in His church in the last days. This church is known as he remnant church which has been discussed in this chapter above. (1 Cor 12:10, Eph 4:11). The Seventh – Day Adventist church believes that the ministry of Ellen G. White meets the specification of (Rev 12:17) in a unique way. In (Eph 4:11), the gifts of the Spirit should continue including that of the Spirit of prophecy.

> "Seventh – Day Adventist do not consider the writings of Ellen G. White as either a substitute for or an addition to the sacred canon for the Adventist, the Bible stands unique and supreme as the test for Christian faith and practice.(see Early Writings 78.) The writings of Ellen G. White serve in her own words, as a "lesser light to lead men and women to the greater light" (Seven – Day Adventist Bible Commentary 1980:877).

The gift of the Spirit of prophecy should still continue even today and this does not mean that everyone becomes a prophet. The tests we discussed above should still apply to whoever claims to be a prophet of God.

4   The Remnant Church

Revelation 12:17 reads; "And the dragon was wroth with the women, and went to make war with the remnant of her seed, which keep the commandments of God and have the testimony of Jesus Christ". We need to look for clues to identify the remnant church. John says,

1) Those who keep the commandments of God and hear the testimony of Jesus.
2) They are entrusted with the proclamation of His final appeal to the world, the three angels' message of Rev 14.
3) Verse 12 of Rev 14 identifies them as people who keep the commandments of God and the faith of Jesus.

Many churches today have nothing to do with the commandment of God, the three angels message and they have bought too many unbiblical things in the teachings of their doctrines. They have added the subtracted a lot from the bible. The remnants have remained with the original doctrine and they teach it as God meant it to be. God will not be forced to understand that which cannot be understood.

If you are among those that are teaching false doctrine, God says if you add or take away he will take away your name from the book of life. Jesus said, "if you love me, keep my commandments". When Jesus was here earth it was the ordinary people who followed him while of the man they were fighting with was the one they were reading about. The scholars of the day were not able to recognize Christ. We should be careful that we should not teach others only to be lost ourselves.

4.1　The Faith of Jesus

The faith of Jesus may mean many things. The faith that Jesus had of the father while on earth or the faith in Jesus that he is the son God, who came into the world. This belief marks God's remnant people today. According Cottrell, "Any church that denies these facts of the Christian faith does not measure up to John's specification". (Cottrell 1963:322).

Faith in Jesus means to take acceptance of the entire Bible as the inspired authority in matters of faith and doctrine. The New and the Old Testament. The remnant will read the prophecies of Daniel and Revelation and preach the everlasting gospel and it will be a missionary minded church. That church will teach all the Bible doctrines taught by all the churches which are Biblical and will keep the law of God and the Sabbath Holy.

4.2　The Commandments of God

Twice John mentions the keeping of the commandments as an identifying characteristic of His remnant people. According to Cottrell, "In the principle and practice they will recognize the continuing validity of all that God has commanded, including all ten precepts of the Decalogue, His unchangeable moral law". (Cottrell 1963:325). The rest of the Christian world today the nine of the ten and that disqualifies them from being the remnant church. Jesus said "If you keep my commandments, you will abide in my love." (II John 5:3).

4.3   Testimony of Jesus

This is the testimony that comes from Jesus. These are the messages borne by His spokesmen, the prophets, to the church. In Revelation, 9:10, John says, "The testimony of Jesus is the spirit of prophecy". As already stated, it is one of the gifts of Holy Spirit. God's last "remnant" will be the direct recipients of inspired messages to guide them in their last great struggles with the powers of evil. False prophets will arise in the last days and Paul says "Do not despite prophesying, but test every thing; hold fast what is good." John wrote, "Do not believe every spirit, but test the Spirits to see whether they are of God." This has already been dealt with in this script.

If you wish to find God's remnant people today, look for a group of people among other things, have a living faith in Jesus, who keep all God's commandments, including the fourth which is Sabbath, who bear consistent witness to the great saving truths of the everlasting gospel, and to whom God has entrusted to prophetic gift in order to prepare them for the crucial events soon to take place.

CHAPTER 5

The Role of the Spirit in the Eshatological Ethics of Revelation

In this last chapter, we will deal with the role of the Spirit in making people ready for the eschaton, the Spirit and the eschatological perspective, the role of the Spirit in the eschatological ethics, the resurrection of the dead and eschatological ethics, the final judgment and eschatological ethics and the Revelation for today in South Africa Conclusion.

5   The Spirit and the Eschatolocal Persperctive

Prophecy in the book of Revelation has reached its climax. The seven Spirits are making the victory of the Lamb effective universally. Bauckham describes it well in the Spirit and the eschatological perspective when he says:

> "We have seen that the varied terminology of the spirits's activity reflects the various aspects of "prophecy" broadly understood. The Spirit mediates the activity of the exalted Christ in and through His church, declaring Christ's word to His people in vision and prophetic oracles, leading the prayers of His people, inspiring His people's missionary

witness to the world. In all of this, the Spirit's role is eschatological, constituting the Christian churches, the community of age to come. As it is from the victory of Christ in His death and resurrection that this eschatological activity of the Spirit in the world derives (5:6), so it is towards the fulfillment of the victory in the eschatological future that the Spirit's activity in and through the churches is directed". (Bauckhan 1993;166).

The eschatological role of the Spirit in the apocalypse is not simply that of predicting the events of the end, but to make it possible for the Christians of the seven churches to bear witness of Jesus, and this could be made possible by directing their thoughts and their lives towards the coming of the Lord for the second time to redeem His own. The point of emphasis was not so much to enable them to foresee the future as to enable them to see their present from the perspective of the future. The implications of this may be illustrated from an examination of the role of the Spirit. God does not want to leave anyone out of the kingdom, but He wants everyone to be saved into the kingdom.

5.1   The Role of the Spirit in the Eschatological Ethics

We will examine two passages in which the Spirit is specifically mentioned. Revelation 22:17 and Revelation 11:3-13. The role of the Spirit is not only limited to these two passages, but can be seen throughout Revelation. The Spirit plays a very important role in the eschaton. It has a great role to play in the ethics of Revelation too.

5.1.1   The Bride in Revelation

The careful identification of the bride is very important, because the bride is not the sum of the Christian communities' observable in the world at the end of the first century: "The churches in Smyrna, Philadelphia and Sardis and the rest. The new Jerusalem is the bride of the lamb that comes down out of heaven from God" (Bauckham 1993:163) (21:2). It is the church at the consummation of history.

The bride is the church which the Lamb when He comes will find ready for His marriage, arrayed in the fine linen of the righteous deeds (19:7 – 8). The white linen is a sign of purity of the church that did not involve itself in harlotry with Babylon, but kept itself pure for the Lamb. The harlotry is the teaching of the false doctrines, the bringing in of man made laws into the church of God. The bride is the church seen from the perspective of the parousia.

The seven churches in the apocalypse were addressed differently from each other. In Laodicea, the Christians are addressed as having "solid clothes" (3:17). This is the contrast of pure linen of the bride. The general unpreparedness for the Lord's coming in Ephesus, Pergamum and Sardis (2:5, 16, 3:3) contrasts with the bride's ardent prayer for he bridegroom's coming (22:7).

The contrast is not really between the unfaithful and the faithful within the churches. It is not the ready and the unready, but it is rather between present eschatological reality, between the churches as they are and the churches as they should be, if they are to take their place at the eschatological nuptial banquet. Every one who hears the prophecy is "invited to the marriage supper" (19:9); all the churches are summoned by the voice of prophecy to become the bride of the Lamb.

The church which is praying for the coming of the Lord in (22:17) is therefore the eschatological church, the church which will be at the parousia. The voice of the Spirit speaking through the prophets, is leading in prayer, for the role of the Spirit is to direct the churches towards their eschatological reality, those that hear the prophecy are then invited to join their own voices to that of the Spirit, the eschatological church becomes a reality. In the congregations at Ephesus, Smyrna or wherever this is becoming a reality. By eliciting this response, the Spirit is making ready the bride for the arrival of the bridegroom.

According to Bauckham:

> "The prayer for the parousia is at the heart of Christians living according to the apocalypse. Christian life must be lived under the spirit's direction towards the eschatological future out of which the Lord is coming... people who join the Spirit's prayer for the parousia are directing their lives in faith towards that promise. The invitation to the thirst is also a call towards the eschatological future" (Backham 1993:168).

The promise of the water of life without price belongs to the new creation (21:6). It is only through the streets of the New Jerusalem where the river of the water of life will flow. There is no taking the water of life without a turning toward the eschatological future. The water of life, the life of a new creation, is available to people at present. The focus of that promise is the Lord's 'I am coming soon' three times repeated in this epilogue to the apocalypse (22:7, 12, 20) and the promise is also the Lord's invitation into the New Jerusalem. The results of abiding in the ethical teaching of Revelation is eternal life. There are rules to be followed in this life and Revelation is built on those rules which are the ethical teaching. Jesus will only take home those who have done the will of the Father. The good bride not the harlot.

5.1.2   The Two Witnesses Prophecy

God's people are going to be redeemed out of the land of Sodom and Gomorrah and Egypt through the Spirit of prophecy, who thus makes plain its real character as a city ripe for judgment. The reference to the Spirit here is in 11:8. the cities that are mentioned here are the cities of confusion, confused by sin so God is going to a city without sin, the new Jerusalem.

The story of the two witnesses is the story about the Bible, the Old and New Testament. These will go through a great test. The story functions as a summon towards the eschatological future. It is a story which creates the future. According to one Bible commentary:

> "This exaltation of the witness has been understood as symbolizing the remarkable popularity that the scriptures have enjoyed since the early 19th century. Soon after the French revolution, various national

Bible societies were established." (the seventh – day Adventist bible commentary 1980, V 7:805).

The British foreign Bible societies were founded in 1804. The American Bible society was founded in 1816. These Bible societies with many others have circulated scripture portions in more than 1,500 languages. In the past one and half century, the scripture, rather than being relegated to oblivion as a scripture guide, has come to enjoy its widest circulation. In modern society the Bible is the widest read and bought book in the cosmos. It is also one of those books that have been translated into many languages more than any other book.

The churches which are to bear this witness are encouraged with a dramatized version of the Lord's word to the church as Smyrna: "Be faithful until death, and I will give you the crown of life.) 2:10). Baukham says:

> "The role of the Spirit in directing Christians towards the parousia and the role of the Spirit in inspiring those who bear the witness of Jesus come together in this story which crystallizes one of the major messages of the prophecy. Bearing the witness of Jesus is a matter of sharing 'in Jesus the persecution and the kingdom and the patient endurance' (1:9): It leads to suffering, rejection and death." (Bauckham 1993:170.

According to the beast's way of how he sees the world, the death of the witness was his victory (11:7). But viewed form the perspective of the parousia, it is the way to life.

The faithful bearing of the witness of Jesus depends on an outlook formed by the hope of the parousia., it is the way of life. The faithful bearing of the witness of Jesus depends on an outlook formed by the hope of the parousia, the death of Christians through persecution called the martyr's victory. (12:11; 15:2). It is victory because there is hope of life after death for those who believe in Christ our Lord and savior.

The eschatological perspective alone creates the paradox in which the invitation to new life is also summons to death. Jesus said that he who loves his life shall lose it and he who does not love his life shall preserve it. It is better to die for a good cause than a bad cause. There is hope in Jesus Christ.

There is also a future dimensions to the story of the witnesses. If we follow the history of Jesus while He was on this earth, we shall find some close connection with the witnesses, e.g. He was resurrected after three days, (an apocalyptic modification of the third day). The place where the Lord was crucified (11:18), is a striking matter of fact, which represents the vision of the apocalypse.

Jesus' life history played a pivotal role in the apocalypse which guaranteed the eschatological future hope. He was crucified then he died, but He is alive for evermore (CF 1:18). This provides the positively model towards the parousia meantime, the way to eternal life comes through death. Our savior had the same experience.

In (11:8) "the great city) which the Spirit identifies as Sodom and Egypt, there is a phrase, where also their Lord was crucified; seems to identify it as Jerusalem, but the Great city is Revelation's otherwise consistent terminology for Babylon (Rome). (14:8;17; 17:18; 18:2, 10, 16, 18 – 19, 21). The Spirit defines present situation seen in eschatological perspective. "In its rejection of Jesus, Jerusalem forfeited the role of holy city (11:2), which often John then transfers to the new Jerusalem (21:2,10)" (Bauckham 1993:172). The story of the two witnesses might have taken place in Jerusalem since Jerusalem did not treat the prophets well. Babylon means the place of confusion and any place that persecutes prophets can be called Babylon.

5.2 The Eschatology and Ethics of the Second Coming of Christ

The Revelation of Jesus Christ, which God gave unto Him, to show unto His servants' things which must shortly come to pass. (1:1). Revelation is a book about the second coming of Jesus Christ. In verse seven we read "Behold He cometh with clouds, and every eye shall see Him" (Rev 1:7).

The role of the Spirit in the second coming of Christ is to reveal to the world the coming of the Lord and the great events before He comes. The calling of the gentiles and Jews to repentance. The Spirit through out John warned of the great apostacy and the great tribulation. The coming Revelation of the Antichrist, the second coming, the manner of the second coming, all these revealed in full by the Spirit in Revelation. All will be judged from the same ethical platform, the law of God.

In conclusion, Christ makes the universal invitation, (22:17 – 20), "And the Spirit and the bride say come, and let him that heareth say, come. And let him that is athirst come, and whosoever will, let him take the water of life freely ...... He which testifieth these things saith, surely I come quickly. Amen. Even so, come Lord Jesus" (Rev 22:20). Jesus promised to send the Spirit, when He left this world and indeed the Spirit is doing His part now.

God's eschatological ethics requires him to keep his promise that he will not do anything without telling it to his servants, the prophets. The parousia is coming and before that, the eschatology, then the coming of the Lord. It is ethical that God will keep his promise and he requires us to respond to his call to come out of Babylon.

5.3   Millenial View and Eschalogical Ethics

There are many views about the millennium, many of which are contradictory. What does the Bible say about this? There are those who say Christ will come before the millennium, they are called premillennialist, and those who say He will come after the millennium are called the postmillennialist. There are also those who do not believe in the millennium called the amillenialists.

Those who believe in the millennium base their belief on Revelation (20: 1 – 7). The Devil will be found for a thousand years, (v 2). He will deceive the nations no more until thousand years is over. The righteous will reign with Christ for a thousand years in heaven. The rest of the dead remain dead for a thousand years, after that the Devil will call them for a battle against the saints and then fire will come down from heaven to consume them.

The millennium is the period between the two resurrections. When Christ shall come the second time, He will take the righteous with Him to heaven and that will be the begging of the millennium. At the end of the millennium, He will come down from heaven with saints as the New Jerusalem descends from heaven. This is the time sin is destroyed forever (1 Cor 15:48 – 58; 1 Thess 4: 13 – 18; Rev 21: 1-15). The Devil's followers are raised to die again and never to be resurrected.

The other theories have no biblical foundation regarding the eschatological millennium. The Bible is specific about the years and the followers of Christ will be with Him for a thousand years, praising and reigning with him, they shall also be judges and priests with Him. Nothing that defiles will enter into the city, either whatsoever worketh abomination, or maketh a lie, but they which are written in the Lamb's book of life. (21:27).

5.4   The Ressurection of the Dead and Eschatological Ethics

When God created human beings he created us to live for ever, but sin came into the world, and death came with it and he made provision through his son to die for all mankind. Death has been on this cosmos ever since, but Christ overcame death from the grave, he arose and now he is alive forever more. he has gone to prepare a place for those who believe in him then he will come again to take them, those who will be found living as well as those who died. They shall all be changed in a moment and death will have no more power over them forever more. (1 Cor 15:50 – 58).

The Old Testament as well as the New Testament talked about the resurrection of the dead e.g. Exk 37: 1 – 14, Psalm 49:15; Prov 23:14 etc. The resurrection will be for the saints, they shall be raised first, then after the millennium the wicked will be raised to be destroyed again. John in (Revelation 20:6), says "Blessed and holy is he that hath part in the first resurrection on such the second death has no power." Missing the first resurrection means everlasting doom.

John tried to warn people of the coming doom, but on the other hand God cannot force people to choose Him. Jesus said "Behold I stand at the door and knock, whoever opens for me, I will come in and sup with him." (3:20). whoever takes part in the second death would have done so by choice. The first death is inherited as a result of sin through Adam and Eve, the second death is by choice, and it can be avoided if God is chosen. Choose ye this day whom ye shall serve (Joshua 24:15).

We serve such a wonderful God who is so good to everyone and he has made all the provision for the salvation of mankind. This is ethically right because God has put the rules, and when they affect him he does not jump them, he gets the punishment, and if we do not do them we get the punishment. If we refuse God's call, we are going to die in our sins.

5.5   The Final Judgement and Eschatological Ethics

When Jesus returns one of the business he will conduct is judgment. Which is known here as the last judgment.

Berkhof says: "The Lord is coming again for the very purpose of judging the living and consigning each individual to his eternal destiny". (Berkhof 1981:728). If there is one business that will be scaring, it is the judgment, it is not easy to be sure of the results of the judgment. The judge will give the verdict and it will be final. We have the choice to make and that is to choose Christ because He will be the judge and our spokesmen to the father. His blood has been shed for us on Calvary.

John says:

> "And I saw a great white throne ... the books were opened: and the dead were judged out of those books according to their works." Rev 20: 11 – 15.

Berkhof talks of the different parts of judgment which are: 1) Cognizance, 2) Promulgation and 3) the sentence. God's judgment will be fair in all respect. He is going to Judge us using his law and we need to know it and keep it to the letter. Paul says that the law is the mirror, it makes us aware of the requirement and the blood of Christ washes away the sins.

5.5.1 Cognizance

God will not just judge us anyhow, He will be a righteous judge who will bring everything to the open. Berkhof says, "God will take cognizance of the state of affairs of the whole past life of human, including even the thoughts and the secret intentions of the heart." (Berkhof 1981:734).

God knows even what is hidden and He will reveal everything so that every one will see that His judgment is fair. (Dan 7:10; Rev 20:12; Malachi 3:16). The book of remembrance will be there too. After God is through with the judgment every body will be satisfied with the verdict of the final judgment. The book of remembrance will be taken out for mankind to satisfy oneself completely.

We have a God who will not just let us be lost, and He has done all in His power to make sure redemption is complete. That is why salvation is free for us but it was not free for God. He emptied heaven for our sake and for us to be lost it will not be God's fault but our own. We have no reason to be lost.

5.5.2   Promulgation

There will be promulgation of the sentence. This day will be a day of wrath, because all must be revealed before the tribunal of the supreme judge (11 Cor 5:10). Justice demands this. "The sentence pronounced to every one will not be secret, it will be publicly proclaimed so that those concerned will know. God's grace and righteousness will shine out in all their splendor". God's grace and righteousness will shine out in all their splendor". (Berkhof 1981:734).

When the sentence has been passed, nobody will have any more questions, because it will be so clear that no one will need further explanation at all. That is how fair God's justice will be. God has been so patient with the Devil, sin and sinners and his cup is full, the time will come when he will not take it anymore and he will call his children home to be with him, and he will destroy sin forever. The signs of Jesus' coming are telling and we are to prepare for Him and get ready.

5.5.3   The Sentence

The law comes first and then if people do not keep it or fail to keep according to the specifications they are charged and Judgment is passed for or against.

"There will be promulgation of the sentence. The day of Judgment is the day of wrath, and of the revelation of the righteous judgement of God, Rom 2:5. All must be revealed before the tribunal of the supreme Judge 11, Cor 5:10. The sense of Justice demands this. The sentence pronounced upon each person will not be secret, will not be known to that person only, but will be publicly proclaimed, so that at least those in any way concerned will know. Thus the righteousness and grace of God will shine out in all their splendor." (Berkhof 1981: 734).

God will bring all works into judgment and for judgment to be fair; it must be open to all. The judgment will divide mankind into two groups, the good and the bad. The will not be the middle of the road. The final state of both has been told, the righteous to everlasting life and the wicked to condemnation. According to the Spirit, the choice is with each individual while they are still alive and before the judgment comes. The ethics of God does not go according to the majority, but the right is right even if one person can do it and the majorities do not, it still remains right.

5.6   The Final State

In this country when you are found guilty you have to serve a prison term or a life sentence, but in other countries is prison term or death sentence. The same applies to the final judgment of this world, which will be the last judgment of all judgments and after that all the judges of this world will be rendered jobless. We need to get serious about God's business because what we are going to go through determines our destiny forever because: "The last judgment determines, and therefore naturally leads on to the final state of those who appear before the judgment seat. Their final state is either one of everlasting misery or one of eternal blessedness," (Berkhof 1981:735).

5.6.1   The Final State of the Wicked

The final destination of the wicked is called hell, 'the lake of fire' (Rev 20:14 – 15). This is the place of eternal punishment, from which Revelation calls its readers to avoid to go to by accepting the invitation of Jesus Christ to eternal life. The final destination for the wicked will be there, the final punishment will be there and the state is which they will continue to exist.

The duration of the punishment according to the Bible is eternal death, and burning last thins with the everlasting fire. The fire of hell is called an "unquenchable fire" Mark 9:43. We have many theories about the final state of the wicked; the reality is that they will not exist in peace in this world or the world to come. We need to make preparations now because when Jesus comes there will be no time to decide. We are warned to be ready at all times because we know not the time or the hour of His coming.

5.6.2   The Final State of the Righteous

This world will come to pass and the new creation will be ushered in. The new creation in which God is going to bring the new heaven and the new earth, where sin shall never be heard off nor seen. This will be the eternal abode of the righteous. Their reward will be eternal life. This life will not only be endless but life in all its fullness.

This is the kind of life we are called to come and enjoy with Jesus. We will forget the pains we have gone through in this world, Jesus will wipe away all tears from our eyes, we will be invited to the marriage supper of the Lamb. What an invitation? The whole Bible is full of guidelines of how to get to heaven and what to do in order to get there, ours is to accept the invitation and then to do the will of the Lord.

5.7   Revelation for Today in South Africa

Revelation is relevant to people living in South Africa today. Its message is timely and relevant to this generation, more so that people are living at the times of the end when earth's history is about to close, the challenges are greater. Revelation contains the doctrines of the last things and as such they must be studied. Christians should work hard to spread the gospel of God's coming kingdom and to bring people to repentance by pointing them to the lamb that takes away the sins of the world. South Africa forms part of the world that must receive the good news or reject it after it after having heard.

This country must take the words written in the book very seriously because it comes to many at a time when people have just tested their independence or political freedom and some are tempted to think that there is no God because of their communistic ideology. This is the right book for South Africans today. The message of judgment should be made known to the people in this country. Jesus must be presented to everyone even the ones in high positions in government, because they also need a savior too. We have no more time to waste.

Conclusion

It has been a great privilege to study the last book of the Bible. The book of prophecy, miracles of the Spirit and the Lamb. Christians need to know this prophecy and then proclaim it to the cosmos. In this book John has guided Christians throughout the ages how Jesus has cared and loved His people. The church has been a constant inspiration to those that watched it though the persecution and the testing times of its history and she has lived to triumph over her enemies. The hope of eternal life inspired her to move forward in faith to reach her destiny. The blessed hope of the church has been the return of the Bridegroom.

The role that the Spirit is playing must be admired in leading the old prophets and the new to write to the churches to rebuke and commend. The seen churches have commendations to either change or continue with their good works in order to prepare for the coming kingdom and this message did not only end up with them, but it has been passed on even to us of the last generation before his arrival. The drama that John has been showing us closes with the beautiful new earth and the glory of the New Jerusalem, the new city of God prepared for the saints.

God came to John to reveal secret things which should give him hope in the hopeless state in which he was in on the Island of Patmos away from everyone else to die a lonely death. He comes to reveal to him that the suffering that he is going through is not compared to the glory that is coming. He takes John by his hand into a vision of the new heavens and the new city whose streets are not ordinary streets, but paved with gold. The sea is not just an ordinary sea, but the sea of glass. John says that sin will never be allowed in there, only those that are written in the lamb's book of life.

The book has taken the church through all kinds of suffering. Those that will endure until the end the same shall be saved. John says that we should hold fast that which we have and let no one take it from our hands, because he that has promised is faithful and he will not tarry, but come to take us home. John says the one who promised is faithful and true to keep his word. A blessing is given to the one who keeps the sayings of this prophecy of the book. The soon return of the savior is promised, He says, "And behold I come quickly; and my reward is with me, to give every man according to his work shall be." (Revelation 22:12).

Many years ago when I was still a small boy we were told that if you read the bible from Genesis, to Revelation you will be mentally disturbed and we were discouraged from reading the book of Revelation. This was a ploy by the Devil to try and discourage people from studying the bible and not come to the knowledge of the saving grace of our Lord Jesus Christ. Many people still do not want to read even though the book of Revelation is an open book and a blessing is pronounced to the one who reads it.

The Devil has brought to us something that will take us from reading the Bible and that is the television he makes sure that our work and responsibilities are increased such that we have no time to read God's word until we are lost to his side. Paul says that nothing should separate us from the love of God (Romans 8:28 – 38).

The last of the seven beatitudes found in Revelation is pronounced: "Blessed are they that do his commandments that they may have the right to the tree of life, and may enter in through the gates into the city." (Revelation 22:14). Suffering and crying may last through the night, but joy comes in the morning. Jesus will bring with Him joy, peace and happiness in our souls.

We must keep God's commandments even though obedience is never a ground of grace, but God's grace is the ground for our obedience. It was through disobedience that our first parents were shut out of Eden their garden home, and prevented from the tree of life. It is only through submission to God's will that man can be reinstated in the paradise of God and again have access to the tree of life. We must do his commandments.

Anderson sums up the throne of God as follows:

> "From that matchless throne of glory flows the wondrous river of life and on its verdant banks of green blooms the fadeless tree of life. Those who reach that land of love shall never know hunger or thirst again. And the good shepherd himself will lead his flock to fountains of living water. What joy to exchange the toil – worn garments of our pilgrimage for the beauteous robes of light!. All the wounds of all the wars, and all the hurts of hate and sin will be forever banished when, "the Lord bindeth up the breach of his people, and healeth the stroke of their wound." Isaiah 30:26." (Anderson 1953: 211).

What a wonderful assurance to the weak and weary pilgrims who are looking forward to their deliveries from the slavery of sin. How wonderful will it be in the company of God and the Patriarchs. Shall we be among them dear friends? You do not want somebody to watch this episode for you, but you want to see it yourself. Will you be able to say with John," Even so, come, Lord Jesus." Revelation 22:20 – 21.

I am inviting every one to read the book of Revelation and enjoy the blessings as I did. John the revelator has already invited readers to read the words written in the book and I am just reminding the readers again and again. The answer is yours and no one will force you to do it, but yourself and your own conscious. If you will be there we will meet there.

We have this hope of the soon coming Savior and without it our lives will be deprived of meaning and comfort. The glorious coming of our Lord is a necessity if our Christian life is to have meaning, courage, comfort, motivation and a hope for a better life to come. Without hope life is meaningless. We have this hope that burns within our hearts, the hope of the coming savior, and the redeemer of mankind.

Hope is not hope if we have seen that which we have hoped for, but if we have not seen, we do wait for it with patience. The Bible says eye has not seen, nor ear heared that which God has prepared for his children. The only way to see is to wait for the coming savior who will soon appear from the eastern skies. I wish I had a tongue of an Angel to warn the world of the coming danger. Amen! Come, Lord Jesus! (Revelation 22:20).

MARANATHA!

BIBLIOGRAPHY

Anderson,   R.A. 1953. UNFOLDING THE
             REVELATION, PACIFIC PRESS
             Publishing Association, Mountain View,
             California.

Bacciocchi, S 1977. FROM SABBATH TO
             SUNDAY. A historical investigation of
             the rise of Sunday observance in early
             Christianity. The Pontifical Gregorian
             University Press, Rome.

.... S. 1986. THE ADVENT HOPE
             FOR HUMAN HOPELESSNESS.
             BLIBLICAL PERSPECTIVES, 230 Lisa
             Lane, Berrien Springs, Michigan 49103,
             U. S.A.

.... S. 1980. DIVINE REST FOR
             HUMAN RESTLESSNESS. BIBLICAL
             PERSPECTIVES, 230 Lisa Lane, Berrein
             Springs, Michigan 49103, U.S.A.

Barclay   W 1959. THE REVELATION OF
             JOHN. (Volume one), The Saint Andrew
             Press, 121 George Street, Edinburg,
             Scotland.

.... W 1959. THE REVELATION OF
            JOHN. (Volume two), the saint Andrews
            Press, 121 George Street, Edinburg,
            Scotland.

Bauckham   R 1993, THE CLIMAX OF
            PROPHECY. Studies on the book of
            Revelation, T & T Clark Ltd, 59 George
            Street, Edinburg H2 2CQ, Scotland.

.... R 1993, THE THEOLOGY OF THE
            BOOK OF REVELATION. Cambridge
            University Press, London, England.

Beek   A 1970, PLAN OF SALVATION. Shutter
            and Shooter, Pietermaritzburg, Grays Inn,
            230 Church street, South Africa.

Berkhof   L 1981, SYSTEMATIC THEOLOGY,
            The Banner of Truth Trust, the Grey
            house, 3 Murrayfield Road, Edinburg
            Eh12 6E1, Scotland

Bettenson   H 1943. DOCUMENTS OF THE
            CHRISTIAN CHURCH. Second
            Edition, Oxford University Press,
            England.

Bruce   F F 1977. THE NEW INTENATIONAL
            COMMENTARY ON THE NEW
            TESTAMENT. William B Eerdmans
            Publishing Company Co., Grand Rapids,
            Michigan, U.S.A.

Cottrell   R F 1963. BEYOND TOMORROW.
            Southern Publishing Association,
            Nashville, Tennessee, U.S.A.

Du Rand	J A 1991. JOHANNINE PERSPECTIVES. AN INTRODUCTION TO THE JOHANNINE WRITINGS. Doornfontein, Perskor book Printers, Johannesburg, South Africa.
Fiorenza	S E 1991. REVELATION. A VISION OF A JUST WORLD. MINNEAPOLIS, Fortress Press, USA.
Goldstein	C 1992. A PAUSE FOR PEACE. Pacific Press Publishing Association, Boise, Idaho, Oshawa, Ontario, Canada.
Hartingsveld	V L 1984. REVELATION TEXT AND INTERPRETATION. William B. Eerdmans publishing Company, Grand Rapida, Michigan, USA.
Harrington	W J 1993. REVELATION. A Michael Glazier book, the Liturgical press, Collegeville, Minnesota, USA.
Haskell	S N 1914. THE CROSS AND ITS SHADOW. Press of South Lancaster Printing Co., South Lancaster, Massachusetts, USA.
Holbrook	F B (Editor) 1992. SYMPOSIUM ON REVELATION – BOOK1. Biblical Research Institute, General Conference of the Seventh – Day Adventist, Printed by the Review and Herald Publishing association, Hagerstown, Maryland 21740, USA.

.... F B (Editor) 1992. SYMPOSIUM ON REVELATION – BOOK 2. Biblical Research Institute, General Conference of the Seventh – Day Adventist, Printed by the Review and Herald Publishing association, Hagerstown, Maryland 21740, USA.

.... F B (Editor) 1986. SYMPOSIUM ON DANIEL – Biblical Research Institute, General Conference of the Seventh – Day Adventist, Printed by the Review and Herald Publishing association, Hagerstown, Maryland 21740, USA.

.... F B (Editor) 1986. THE SEVENTY WEEKS, LEVITICUS AND THE NATURE OF PROPHECY. Biblical Research Institute, General Conference of the Seventh – Day Adventist, Printed by the Review and Herald Publishing association, Hagerstown, Maryland 21740, USA.

.... F B (Editor) 1989. ISSUES IN THE BOOK OF HEBREWS. Biblical Research Institute, General Conference of the Seventh – Day Adventist, Printed by the Review and Herald Publishing association, Hagerstown, Maryland 21740, USA.

.... F B (Editor) 1989. DOCTRINE OF THESACTUARY. A HISTORICAL SURVEY. Biblical Research Institute, General Conference of the Seventh – Day Adventist, Printed by the Review and Herald Publishing association, Hagerstown, Maryland 21740, USA.

Hyde G M 1978. RAGS TO RIGHTEOUSNESS. Pacific Press Publishing Association, Mountain View, California, USA.

Jemison H T 1955. A PROPHET AMONG YOU. Pacific Press Publishing Association, Mountain View, California, USA.

Mealy W J 1992. AFTER THE THOUSAND YEARS. (RESSURECTION AND JUDGMENT IN REVELATION 20). Sheffield Academic Press, England, United Kingdom.

Michaels R J 1992. INTERPRETING THE BOOK OF REVELATION. Baker book house Company, Grand Rapids, Michigan, USA.

Mounce R H 1977. THE BOOK OF REVELATION.William B. Eerdams Publishing Company, Grand Rapids, Michigan, USA.

Pelikan J 1978. THE GROWTH OF MEDIEVAL THEOLOGY (600 – 1300). The University of Chicago Press, Chicago, USA.

Prevost   J P 1993. HOW TO READ THE
                 APOCALYPSE. Novalis, University
                 Saint – Paul, Ottawa, Canada.
Ramsay   W M 1994. THE LETTERS TO THE
                 SEVEN CHURCHES. Hendrickson
                 Publisher, Peabody Massachusetts, USA.
Rowland   C 1993. REVELATION. Epworth Press,
                 1 Central Buildings, West minister,
                 London, Great Britain.
Schnackenburg R 1962. THE MORAL TEACHINGS
                 OF THE NEW TESTAMENT. The
                 Seabury Press, New York, USA.
Schrage   W 1988. THE ETHICS OF THE
                 NEW TESTAMENT. Fortress Press,
                 Philadelphia, USA.
Shea   W H 1992. SELECTED STUDIES ON
                 PROPHETIC INTERPRETATION.
                 Printed by the Review and Herald
                 Publishing Association, Hagerstown, MD
                 21740, USA.
Venden   M 1993. GOD SAYS, BUT I THINK.
                 Pacific Press Publishing Association,
                 Boise, Idaho, Oshawa, Ontario, Canada.
....   M 1983. TO KNOW GOD. (A
                 FIVE – DAY PLAN). Review and Herald
                 Publishing Association, Washington DC.
                 20039 – 0555, Hagerstown, USA.
Van Daalan   DH 1986. A GUIDE TO
                 REVELATION. Cambridge University
                 Press, London, Great Britain.

Wall	W R 1991. NEW INTERNATIONAL BIBLICAL COMMENTARY ON REVELATION. Hendrickson Publisher, Peabody, Massachusetts, USA.
Wieland	R J 1988. THE GOSPEL IN REELATION. All Africa publications, Southern Publishing Association, Kenil Worth, Cape Town, South Africa.
Wijnsaarda	J 1988. THE SPIRIT IN JOHN. Town house press, Wilmington, Delaware, USA.
White	E G 1911. ACTS OF THE APOSTLES. Pacific Press Publishing Association, Mountain View, California, USA.
....	E G 1899. LIFE AT ITS BEST. Pacific Press Publishing Association, Mountain View, California, USA.
....	E G 1981. UNIVERSE IN CONFLICT. Pacific Press Publishing Association, Mountain View, California, USA.
....	E G 1858. SPIRITUAL GIFTS. VOLUME ONE. Review and Herald Publishing Association, Washington DC, 20039 – 0555, Hagerstown, M. D. USA.
....	E G 1858. SPIRITUAL GIFTS. VOLUME TWO. Review and Herald Publishing Association, Washington DC, 20039 – 0555, Hagerstown, M. D. USA.
Wilson	L 1994. THE REVELATION OF JESUS. SOUTHERN AFRICAN EDITION, Southern publishing Association, Cape Town, South Africa.

1988	Family Bible: Authorized OR King James version, Red letter edition, De ore and Sons, Inc. Wichita, Kansas, USA.
1980 ©	Seventh – day Adventist Bible Commentary, Vol 7, Review and Herald Publishing Association, Washington DC, 20039 – 0555, Hagerstown, M. D. 21740, USA.
1966	Kurt Aland, Mathew Black, Carlo M. Martini, Bruce M. Mertzger and Wikgren Allen (Editors). THE GREEK NEW TESTAMENT. The third Edition, United Bible Societies Press, West Germany.

NEW CONCISE BIBLE DICTIONERY, EDITOR.
Derek Williams, Intervarsity Press, 38 De Montfort Street, Leicester Leifgp, England.

My eldest sister, my twin brother and me
at a wedding in Natal, South Africa.

Paul, Maureen, Tsiko, Thikho, Tshidzwa and Tshedza.
These are the names according to birth right.

Pandelani Paul Mbedzi

Printed in the United States
By Bookmasters